RONALD KNOX
THE PRIEST
THE WRITER

RONALD KNOX

THE PRIEST
by *Thomas Corbishley, S.J.*

THE WRITER
by *Robert Speaight*

SHEED AND WARD
New York

© *Sheed & Ward, Inc., 1965*

Part I of this book was first published in England under the title *Ronald Knox the Priest*, © Thomas Corbishley, S.J., 1964.

> Nihil obstat: Joannes M. T. Barton, S.T.D., L.S.S.
> Censor Deputatus
>
> Imprimatur ✠ Georgius L. Craven,
> Epūs Sebastopolis, Vic. Gen.
>
> Westmonasterii, Die 24a Aug. 1964

Library of Congress Catalog Card Number 65-20864

Manufactured in the United States of America

CONTENTS

I

RONALD KNOX THE PRIEST

by Thomas Corbishley, S.J.

FOREWORD

IT IS NOT without misgiving and largely under pressure from those whose judgement I value that this sketch of Ronald Knox's priestly vocation and activities has been undertaken. Although Mr. Waugh, in the preface to his own "official life," surmises that his work "will prove to be the forerunner of many weightier studies," the very thoroughness with which he has told the story of Ronald's exterior life makes it difficult for anyone to follow him. Fortunately, this slight volume cannot be thought of as a "weightier study." It may perhaps supplement, in this or that detail, the fuller account given by Mr. Waugh. It cannot be regarded as in any sense an alternative Life.

Yet some justification for it may be found in two sentences from that same preface:

I knew him primarily as a man of letters rather than as a priest.

If I have made too much of Ronald's tribulations it is because he hid them, and they must be known to anyone who seeks to appraise his achievement.[1]

[1] *Monsignor Ronald Knox,* © Evelyn Waugh, 1959 (Boston: Little, Brown and Company).

Unlike Mr. Waugh, I knew him primarily as a priest, even whilst I appreciated his achievement as a writer. And if the second sentence just quoted implies a conscious effort to emphasize a not unimportant element in Ronald's experience, that element may be given an exaggerated significance if it is not seen in the context and framework of Ronald's religious and spiritual training. We shall arrive at a balanced appreciation of the man if we study not only the causes and circumstances of those tribulations but also the spirit in which he tried to accept them.

Any priest will be all too conscious that his personal qualities fall far short of the message he seeks to deliver. Temperamental difficulties may to some degree extenuate his shortcomings. But unless he is seen to be making a constant effort to struggle with those difficulties, the validity of his preaching must be called in question. For the priest is much more than a professional man. Ronald said:

Sanctity is not a work done; it is a life lived.

The same can and should be said of the priesthood.

That is why the theme of this brief analysis is the priesthood as the central reality in terms of which everything about Ronald must be evaluated. The first time I set eyes on him— long before I was a priest myself—he was in the pulpit. After I had come to know him intimately, the basis of our friendship was our common vocation.

The better I came to know and understand him, the more did I come to appreciate the way in which the fact of his priesthood dominated his whole outlook. Even his literary activity was almost entirely controlled by his responsibilities as a priest. The apparent exception of his detective stories is not really at variance with this statement. He told me himself that his reason for writing them was that the royalties on them went to support him as chaplain at Oxford. "I used to write one during the Long Vacation, and the £600 or so it brought in kept me for the rest of the year."

Yet, because he was such a delightful companion, such a considerate host, it was possible for the casual acquaintance or the occasional visitor to fail to appreciate the deep and strong reality of his spiritual life. He was always prepared to accommodate himself, to direct the conversation along the lines which would be most welcome to his company. It was in the intimacy of private dialogue that he revealed most completely where his personal interests really lay.

This small tribute, then, is paid by a priest to a fellow priest, whose greatest achievement may well have been that, far beyond the confines of the seminary, he made an outstanding contribution to the education of countless priests—not merely through his retreats to the clergy, but still more through the example he set as preacher, pastor and man of God.

I

SEED-TIME

THE LIFE OF SANCTITY is the story of an alliance—the alliance between an earthbound creature and the time-transcending grace of God. Yet, however mysterious the theologian finds the workings of that grace to be, he encourages us to bear in mind that its effect is to heighten and intensify the natural qualities of the creature. The uniqueness of the individual remains and is emphasized by what we call his "correspondence" with grace—a felicitous term, since it implies that, in a double sense, there is that in man which is adapted to, which corresponds with, the power of God working in him.

Hence there is no reason why the biographer of any person striving towards sanctity should not use the sort of historical method or psychological approach which he would equally use were he writing a "secular" biography. God keeps secret his share in the alliance; even the other partner can never be sure about it. All he is conscious of are the impulses of nature and his own efforts to grow towards the ideal his conscience sets before him. The raw material of his spiritual achievement is to be found in the elements of physical heredity, the psychological conditioning of early environment and education, the social and cultural background of his formative years and that mysterious result of all this which, for want of a better word, we can only call temperament.

With all this in mind, then, we turn to trace the story of Ronald Knox's psychological inheritance and personal development. From the great mass of information and evidence available, any selection must of necessity be conditioned by the personal predispositions and even prejudices of the selecting mind; and since no human being presents himself in precisely the same way to his acquaintances and intimates (these, perhaps, least of all), the resulting portrait is bound to be unbalanced and to some extent misleading. Yet since, whatever else he may have been, Ronald Knox was by chosen calling and by deliberate training first and foremost a priest and a man of God, it seems at least probable that a study which emphasizes these aspects of his career will be essentially truer than one which treats them as of minor significance.

Overmuch emphasis need not be laid on heredity. For, though it is true that Ronald was descended from bishops through his mother as well as through his father, who was himself a bishop, only one of his three brothers took orders. The other two seem to have shown little concern for matters ecclesiastical or religious, whilst Wilfred's Modernist and Liberal outlook was wholly opposed to the scrupulous orthodoxy of his younger brother. (In later life, when he wanted to propound some rather *outré* interpretation of a biblical passage, he would preface his suggestion with the words: "If I were my brother Wilfred, I would say . . .")

Already the mystery of man's response to environmental grace is adumbrated. Why, from a household that was the home of a future bishop, presided over, after his first wife's death, by the daughter of an Anglican canon, should the children take such diverse paths in life? Ronald himself was to hint at the problem without offering a suggested solution.

I cannot imagine circumstances better calculated to impress the mind with that form of Protestant piety, which the modern world half regrets and half derides as "old-fashioned" . . . It is easy to make capital out of such exterior manifestations; and those who, having been brought up in such surroundings, have subsequently changed their views, are often at pains to ascribe all their later developments to a sense of revolt from a system described as sombre and inhuman . . . I suspect in all this a merely literary falsity of retrospect; certainly in my own case, apart from any question of piety, candour compels me to admit that I neither then found nor have since managed to persuade myself that I found, anything repulsive or frightening in such a religious atmosphere. Hell was part of those beliefs, like death; neither death nor hell dwells with any morbid fixity in the mind of a normal child. Rather the personal love which God devotes to us, the ever-surprising miracle of his Redemption, the permanent ease of access to the glorified Saviour—these are the central characteristics of Evangelical devotion, and these its formative influences . . . I believed that I was continually under the eye of a watchful God, just in exacting punishment; but I do not think the consciousness either weighed me down or encouraged scrupulosity.[1]

Was this, in turn, "merely literary falsity of retrospect"? Almost certainly not. For one of the most marked character-

[1] *A Spiritual Aeneid,* New Edition with a Preface by Evelyn Waugh (New York: Sheed and Ward, 1958), p. 5.

istics of Ronald's life was its homogeneity. There were, in his career, moments of crisis, the occasional agony of decision. Yet, as we look at the completed story, we see, not a zigzag course, or a succession of discrete phases. Rather we seem to be watching a natural, almost an inevitable, development, the apparently unforced blossoming of qualities somehow inherent in the child. Clearly, none of those who shared Ronald's early experiences in the last decade of the nineteenth century could have foreseen without a sense of shock the progress by which he was to become one of the luminaries of the Catholic Church and to end his days as a Protonotary Apostolic to the Bishop of Rome. In the Evangelical climate he has described, such a shock would have been inevitable. But those who knew him after his conversion cannot feel that his life was broken at that point; it was, at every level, completed.

His early environment was wholly ecclesiastical. When he was born in 1888 his father held a living at Kibworth in Leicestershire, and after the mother of the six children (of which Ronald was the youngest) died in 1891, Wilfred and Ronald spent the next four years with another clerical uncle. The uncle was a bachelor, but his establishment included his mother and three sisters, who, though they could not compensate for the loss of Ronald's mother, could at least ensure that he would not feel an orphan. He has insisted that his childhood was a happy one, and there seems little reason to doubt his word. There are those who have thought that his later manifest love of young children was a sequel to his own lack of mother-love in childhood. But not a few bachelors who have enjoyed a normal childhood have also been fond of children.

The fact is that he responded to affection wherever it was

displayed, and the unselfconscious friendliness of children easily won his heart. It was easier for them than for their elders
to break through the reserve which surrounded him to the
end. Having given them his affection in their early years, he
did not withdraw it as they grew up, and many of them learnt
to appreciate in adult life the qualities of mind and heart
which they cannot have guessed at in those early days.

In 1894 his father advanced further up the ladder of ecclesiastical preferment by becoming rector of the most important parish in Birmingham, archdeacon of that city and
Suffragan Bishop of Coventry. More important for his own
personal happiness and for the general welfare of his family,
he married again in the spring of the following year. Reunited
to his brothers and sisters, Ronald, for all his literary pre-
cocity—his productions at this time included a Latin drama
and an Horatian ode—was boy enough to become a fierce
partisan of the local football team, Aston Villa.

At the age of eight he entered the preparatory school of
Summer Fields in North Oxford, from which he proceeded
four years later to Eton, first in his election to College. At
both places he was not only outstanding as a scholar; he was
popular with his fellows, with a popularity which depended,
not on athletic prowess, as it so often does, but clearly on his
own personal qualities—that combination of modesty, friendliness and humour which were to endear him to so many
others throughout his life. The friends he made at Summer
Fields and Eton were to remain his friends to the end, though
all too many of them were to be taken from him in the slaugh-
ter of the first Armageddon.

This great gift for friendship which was to be one of the
most obvious features of his life was due to his possession of

those natural endowments which lie at the root of the supernatural virtue of charity. Nor is it true, as has been alleged,
that he cultivated friendships in the more exalted circles of
society. To anyone who knew him, the mere suggestion is
ludicrous. Not only were his friends to be found at every
level of the population, and not least amongst the parochial
clergy, but it was they who sought his friendship rather than
he theirs. He responded quickly and readily to any manifesta-
tion of understanding sympathy, intelligent appreciation of
his work or simple affection. He was absolutely normal in that
he liked to be liked, and that he rejoiced in the company of
those who were "nice and easy to get on with." He enjoyed
intelligent conversation; but he also enjoyed playing games
with children. In his more robust days, he liked fooling about
on pogo-sticks and garden-rollers, punting and canoeing with
undergraduates, exploring the subterranean streams of Oxford. His range of friendships was indeed remarkable. He
moved with ease in the most distinguished company. But he
made no parade of this, nor was there anything remotely approaching snobbishness in his attitude to others. He was utterly unassuming.

That he should have passed through the triumphs of Eton
and Oxford without developing the slightest air of self-
importance is a remarkable indication of his unfailing modesty. For his career both at Eton and Oxford was triumphant
almost beyond description. Academic distinction was matched
by a remarkable measure of personal popularity. In the field
of learning, his Eton days were a succession of prizes and
scholarships gained, crowned by his winning the first scholarship to Balliol, which was then at the height of its fame as
the most intellectually distinguished college at Oxford. His

personal qualities won him the scarcely less coveted distinction of election to "Pop"—that self-perpetuating society of those who regard themselves, and are regarded, as Eton's elite.

It is almost certainly true that for Ronald Knox his school-days were indeed the happiest days of his life. His success in the academic field has become almost legendary. The list of scholarships and prizes he gained need not be given here, and it will be enough to quote from the letter announcing that he had won the first scholarship to Balliol.

His knowledge is so remarkable that we feel he should do little work after he has got the Newcastle—in fact one of my colleagues suggests that he had better go a voyage round the world and forget it all.[2]

In addition to all this there was the immense satisfaction of belonging to a group of friends who were, by any standards, remarkable young men.

He was at the same time maturing spiritually. He had, as we know, been devout from his earliest days, but perhaps until his sixteenth year he had taken his religion entirely for granted. Given his home background, it was inevitable that this should happen. But there is no evidence that he was precocious spiritually, as he undoubtedly was intellectually. He had already come to take it for granted that he would enter the Anglican ministry, but probably in much the same spirit as that in which a son of a military family takes it for granted that he will enter the Army. Yet he gave up this idea for a time, although it returned when he began to take a genuine interest in the Oxford Movement. Otherwise:

[2] Evelyn Waugh, *op. cit.*, pp. 59-60.

The only memory I have of strong spiritual feelings in my first years at Eton is that of a violent, almost hysterical penitence when my place in the term's order was lower than it should have been; I have no doubt it was salutary, but I am afraid the subject of my repentance was characteristic.[3]

Even so:

. . . It is only fair to my early religious education to say that, under God, I think I should have gone up to Oxford as a believer and a regular communicant even if I had not come under the influences which are to be described in the next chapter.[4]

He then goes on to tell of the effect on him of reading Wakeman's *History of the Church of England*, leading up, as it did, to the climax of the Oxford Movement. The reading of this book gave something of historical depth to the superficial, yet genuine, influence of Benson's *The Light Invisible*, with its first introduction to his knowledge of the "Catholic system." It was from this point that he was to date his "conversion"; but his conversion to something as yet only vaguely apprehended. A growing interest in the Tractarian Movement coincided with an awakening interest in Gothic architecture, side by side with an enthusiasm for the Pre-Raphaelites. At this time, too, began his Ritualistic phase, though this was consciously related to his Tractarianism.

It is easy to see in all this a first step on the Romeward path; and so, in effect, it proved to be. But is it possible to interpret this stage in his development in terms of temperamental idiosyncrasies? Well, first of all, this was happening in his

---

[3] *A Spiritual Aeneid*, p. 26.
[4] *A Spiritual Aeneid*, p. 30.

seventeenth year, an age which has ever looked for Causes to espouse. There was, too, in Ronald, a romantic element which never left him, from the early days when, after having been a "Roundhead" because his hair was straight and he envied his brother's curls, he "played traitor to the standards of Dunbar." To the end of his life he remained an ardent monarchist. He confesses, further, that he always took a "Catonic pleasure in the defeated cause."

It is hardly surprising, then, that the knowledge that there actually was a Cause "for which clergymen had been sent to prison, a Bishop censured, noble lives spent" should have fired the imagination of one who had already come under the spell of the essential Catholicity of the Eton tradition—"the memory of the pious founder," the "strong sense of the patronage of the Mother of God."

Her name was part of our title; her lilies figured on our coat of arms; the blue of her robe you could see daily on the blazers of the Eight and the caps of the Eleven.[5]

But all this might have been no more than a passing emotion. What mattered was its abiding effect on his personal religious practice. Every Sunday he communicated, and during his last year at school (the eighteenth year of his age) he occasionally managed to communicate on weekdays; he attended Evensong with increasing regularity; his private devotions he stimulated with the help of "one or two religious prints," later to be joined by a small crucifix.

More significant still, and something less common even amongst more pious schoolboys, was the practice of mild

[5] *A Spiritual Aeneid*, p. 41.

forms of asceticism, including the time when, for a period of six weeks whilst a friend lay dangerously ill of typhoid, he ate nothing at meals except bread and butter. (His schoolfellows regarded this simply as a criticism of the quality of the food provided.) Most remarkable of all was the vow of celibacy which he took at the age of seventeen. He was not, he insists, influenced by a "sense of oppression about purity." Rather it was an explicit recognition of a dawning vocation. He must have "power to wait upon the Lord without impediment," and he was aware that his sensitive and affectionate nature would crave the sympathy and support of a happy marriage. Such was not for him. "I have an errand on a stony way" is the opening line of a sonnet which he wrote at this time, a sonnet which expresses his consciousness of being called to a way of life that was to make demands on him, to the exclusion of those human ties which, of themselves good and honourable, he recognized already as not for him. The pathway to the full Catholic priesthood was to be wide open.

This may be the best opportunity for discussing his attitude to sex. It is true that, as Mr. Waugh says, he was "peculiarly reluctant to mention any question of sex even in its most impersonal aspect," and this may well be due, initially, to the early conditioning during the years after his mother's death when he was so much in the company of maiden aunts. It is true that, like Queen Victoria, he was not amused by the coarser type of smoking-room story. It is true that, at school and elsewhere, he seems to have been protected from the impact of grosser temptations.

. . . I believe it possible at an ordinary house in an ordinary school for an ordinary boy, though he may hear much obscene conversation and much scandalous gossip, to go through his school time without having the moral evils, which sometimes lie beneath the surface, thrust upon his notice. I knew people who were by repute immoral; the conventions of our society, as well as charity, demanded that I should give them the benefit of the doubt.[6]

But it is highly probable that his reluctance to talk about sexual difficulties, even in sermons, even in retreats, was largely due to his general desire to emphasize the positive aspect of the Christian life, as we shall come to see in a later chapter. For the moment it is sufficient to suggest that here, once again, we have an example of a native fastidiousness providing the basis for a later spiritual and supernatural development.

It is impossible then, looking back at this stage, not to think that these first eighteen years of Ronald's life were a providential initiation, a preparation for all that was to follow. The Evangelical background laying the foundations of a deeply personal religion; the classical and historical education preparing him for both the brilliant apologetic and the not less brilliant literary achievement; the growing interest in, and knowledge of, the Anglo-Catholic movement in the Church of England—all this was to be reinforced and developed during the next stage of his growth.

In his own account of his four years at Balliol (1906–10), he divides his self-analysis into a consideration of "secular influences" and an examination of his "religious development." Of the former, it is perhaps enough to suggest that a career so outstanding in every way cannot but have established in him an assurance and a self-confidence, which were

[6] *A Spiritual Aeneid*, p. 43.

nevertheless entirely compatible with that extraordinary modesty and lack of aggressiveness which were amongst his most obvious characteristics. He was to confess in later years that, possibly because he had been the youngest of four brothers, he always felt that there must be something in other people's objections to his views. Yet no one who swayed the Union as he could sway it, who could number amongst his closest friends some of the most remarkable men of his generation, who carried off every academic prize that was open to him—his one comparative failure was his Second in Mods —no one could have such a series of successes to his name and not feel intellectually and socially secure.

A first in Greats left me neither a professional philosopher nor a professional historian; but it left me with a fierce love of sifting evidence and the power of not being fascinated into acquiescence when superior persons talked philosophy at me.[7]

The danger of an Oxford career so successful following on the extraordinary achievement at Eton might well have turned his head, made him intellectually arrogant, turned him into a "superior person." Once again, it might be claimed, grace came to build on the foundations laid by his earliest experiences. The clue is given in a precious study by Mgr. Vernon Johnson in a privately circulated memoir.

In the midst of all this adulation Ronald Knox remained quite unmoved and utterly unspoilt. What was the secret which kept him always so charmingly modest amid this hurricane of fame? His racy wit and inveterate love of a joke had indeed quickly

[7] *A Spiritual Aeneid*, p. 55.

earned for him the reputation of being an *enfant terrible*, flippant and superficial. Little did these people know of the private personal life which lay behind this brilliance and which he was at such pains to keep completely hidden.

Two incidents will reveal it. In the early morning, often after a dazzling success at some great debate at the Oxford Union, he would slip out of Balliol across St. Giles to Pusey House. There, together with our little group, he would make his communion quite unconcerned, just as friendly and just as much at ease with us, most of whom were very ordinary, as he was with the brilliant company of the night before. At least twice in the week he would be found making his communion in this manner, no mean achievement when one realizes what an undergraduate's evening usually can be.

The second occasion was when he had just finished his papers for the Ireland, Oxford's greatest classical prize. A few days before the result was due to be published he came and begged me to spend the intervening time with him in retreat at the Cowley Fathers so that he might be ready to accept the result properly whichever way it went. On the last morning of the little retreat it was announced that R. A. Knox had won the coveted prize . . .

It is true that, in his own account of these years, Ronald seems more anxious to discuss his "ecclesiastical" developments than the deepening of his personal religious life. Yet if he spoke at times as if it was all a matter of external form, ritual, furniture and the like, it is quite clear that he was concerned with these primarily, if not solely, because of their effect on people's spiritual lives. His very first visit to Caldey Abbey (in 1909) makes this clear. Whilst he affirms that he "must have measured the satisfactoriness" of the various churches he came across "by the degree to which they approximated to the island ideal," he was not by any means referring solely to outward appearances.

The value of devotions to the Blessed Sacrament was now a clear article of my creed, and was to become the chief cause for which I was prepared to do battle.[8]

More and more he was coming to accept those practices which are native to the Catholic mind, even "to treasure details of worship because Rome practised them"; yet he still hoped, as he went on hoping, that all this could be a means of revivifying the spiritual life of the Church of England. Of its implications for his own allegiance he still seemed unaware.

When he went down from Balliol in 1910 it was merely to go next door to Trinity, where he had been offered and had accepted a fellowship, with a view to his succeeding, in two years' time, the chaplain who was to leave at that date. Meanwhile, his ordination to the diaconate in 1911 meant for him the beginning of that long and enormously successful career as a preacher which must form the subject-matter of a special chapter. For our present purpose it is sufficient to note that his activities at this time seem to have been concerned partly with attempts to deepen the spiritual awareness of the members of his congregations, partly to resist the growing influence of Modernist Higher Criticism in the Church. At the purely intellectual level he was assisted in this by his acute realisation of the inadequacy of the "critical" method as applied to the works of Homer. As a joke, he applied the technique of the method to the Sherlock Holmes saga. It was taken by many of those who heard him read the paper as an attack on the

[8] *A Spiritual Aeneid*, p. 71.

whole school of the Higher Critics. Almost accidentally, it might seem, he found himself cast as a defender of traditional views against the new tendency.

But we need not think that it was all purely accidental. For, in attacking the inerrancy and inspiration of the Bible, the critics were, in his view, manifesting a frivolity and irresponsibility of outlook which struck at the very foundations of the Faith. Paradoxically, the solemn pedants were, fundamentally, far less serious-minded than the apparently flippant and facetious young Knox. For his mockery was directed to the defence of truth; their pomposity was an expression of an attitude of mind which held that scholarship was the touchstone of true religion. Has there ever been a more devastating reply to the whole rationalist approach than the ingenious, entertaining and skilfully sustained satire in the manner of Dryden, *Absolute and Abitofhell*.

> When suave Politeness, temp'ring bigot Zeal,
> Corrected *I believe* to *One does feel*.

As he was to write in 1913:

The argument has been, not that we should distrust hypotheses because of their uncertainty, but that we should distrust them because of the certainty with which inconsiderate people have held them . . . It is not merely that they are insecure avenues to truth; my complaint is that they contain definite provocation to error. And on the ground of this constant temptation, of which I am myself fully conscious, if I could not preach the Christian faith in its fullness on a basis of absolute *a priori* certainty, I would give up preaching it altogether.[9]

[9] *Some Loose Stones* (London: Longmans, 1913), p. 2.

He possessed all, and more than all, the dialectical skill and linguistic ability to make him, had he been so inclined, one of the most ruthless of destructive critics. He was saved from being merely clever by the deeper insight into the realities of religious faith which was always such a marked characteristic of so much of his writing. It was his genuine goodness, his deep-rooted respect for sacred truth, which preserved him from succumbing to the temptation of which he was "fully conscious." He was to become one of the most persuasive of advocates for the fullness of Christian truth, with a simplicity and directness of argument which may well suggest that he had always found it easy to believe. But there are hints here and there in his writings which clearly imply that he had to struggle for that faith which seemed so unfailingly serene.

At any time since I was seventeen I have had "temptations against the faith," not so much against particular articles in the creed as against the whole system of religion: the existence of God and the survival of the soul after death have always been the doctrines which, in this sense, presented difficulties to me . . .[10]

Or again,

To others, belief is a burden which must be shouldered. They recognise it as an intellectual obligation, but it does not come natural to them or sit easily on them; they have to go on telling themselves "This must be true."[11]

[10] *A Spiritual Aeneid*, pp. 53-4.
[11] *Lightning Meditations*, © *Evelyn Waugh*, 1959 (New York: Sheed and Ward, 1959), p. 54.

Mr. Waugh has said, with perfect justice: "Genius and sanctity do not thrive except by suffering." But it is probable that the sufferings which tempered Ronald Knox's spirit were those which he endured during these years when he was growing daily into a deeper and fuller realization of the rich significance of the Christian faith. If he was to be such a powerful source of light and comfort in the years to come, it was certainly because he had forged in the fires of his own experience the weapons which he was to wield with practised skill. In all the Virgilian references with which the *Spiritual Aeneid* is studded he does not quote—nor, clearly, could he— the words of Dido to Aeneas:

Haud ignara mali miseris succurrere disco.

(Acquaintance with adversity is the school in which I learn to succour the distressed.)[12]

We are no longer concerned with the controversial years that preceded Ronald's reception into the Catholic Church. They have their interest for the historian of the Oxford Movement. For the historian of Ronald's personal development, probably the most significant passage in his own account is the brief paragraph:

Well before the end of the first week [of the two weeks he spent at Farnborough Abbey, where he was to be received] I knew that grace had triumphed. I neither expected nor received any sensible supernatural illumination: I did not have to take my spiritual temperature, "evaluate" my "experiences," or proceed in

12 *Aeneid*, 1. 630.

any such quasi-scientific manner. I turned away from the emotional as far as possible, and devoted myself singly to the resignation of my will to God's Will . . . In the mere practice of religion, in the mere performance of these (very informal) exercises, I knew that it was all right.[13]

And, a little later: "I know now that as an Anglican I was trying to force God's Hand."[14]

And so, on 22 September 1917, Ronald Knox became a Catholic.

He came into the Church exhausted by the long struggle to clarify his mind about the road he must take, an exhaustion immensely increased by the emotional stresses of those years of war, which took away from him most of the friends of his Eton and Balliol days. The vow he had taken at Eton had prepared him spiritually for the loss of human affection; but he felt deeply the successive blows inflicted by the casualty lists, culminating in the most grievous loss of all, the death of his dearest friend, Guy Lawrence, in August 1918. "When I heard about Guy Lawrence, I was completely numbed to all feeling for about five days," he was to write in a letter to another friend.

Already he had begun to experience the kindliness and consideration which he almost invariably received at the hands of the Catholic authorities. Cardinal Bourne, to whom Ronald presented himself soon after his reception, took the unusual step of exempting him from the rigours of the normal seminary training, even the mitigated rigours of the Beda, and left him free to arrange his own theological studies. Ronald was at

[13] *A Spiritual Aeneid,* p. 214.
[14] *A Spiritual Aeneid,* p. 226.

the time working in Military Intelligence, and the Cardinal suggested that he should live at the Oratory, to familiarize himself with Catholic ways, devoting such time as he could to theological pursuits. Few outside the ranks of the clergy will appreciate the remarkable liberality of such an arrangement, sensible and reasonable as it undoubtedly was.

This is an appropriate moment to discuss the allegation made, sometimes by Catholics, more frequently by those who have remained outside, that Ronald Knox's conversion was the beginning of a succession of humiliations and frustrations which made it impossible for him to deploy fully his remarkable literary and academic abilities. Sometimes a parallel is drawn with the frequent and prolonged disappointments which saddened the life of John Henry Newman. The parallel is totally lacking in substance. It is true that, for one reason or another, Ronald had to put up with vexatious misunderstandings in relatively minor matters; it is true that he was sensitive to criticism, and sometimes gave expression to his disappointment in language which, to those who did not know him well, might suggest a thoroughly disgruntled and disappointed man. But the scale of his tribulations was scarcely to be compared with Newman's. Newman wins our sympathy because, we feel, he was unfairly treated. Ronald Knox, we feel, suffered not so much from outside opposition as from a sense of failure which sprang, as much as anything, from the very demands he made on himself.

And again, if we are to appreciate aright the wide divergence between John Henry Newman and Ronald Knox we must bear in mind the sheer gaiety, the capacity for laughter, even for laughing at himself, which Ronald possessed and Newman certainly did not. Already in 1917, whilst he was still outside the Church, he wrote of himself: "Fortunately I had too much capacity for laughing at myself to fall into the error of posing as a martyr."

It was a gift he never lost.

When, in December 1918, he was released from his duties at the War Office, he was asked by Cardinal Bourne to go to St. Edmund's, the diocesan seminary. Whilst continuing his theological studies and waiting for ordination to the priesthood, he was to help with the teaching in the school. He would be able to continue his own writing (it was the period during which he indulged in much popular journalism) and his week-ends would be free. Again, one is struck by the exemption from traditional discipline to which the theological student is normally subjected.

St. Edmund's was poles apart from Eton; the masters far removed from the senior common-room at Trinity. Yet, with the adaptability which was one of the constant surprises to those who thought they knew him well, he settled down cheerfully to the new conditions and made friends as genuine and loyal as any he had ever known. He was no longer capable of the ardours of youth, but he often spoke with genuine affection of those whom he had known there; in their turn they, quite simply, loved him. It is not at all unlikely that, before his arrival, his reputation must have seemed a daunting one. His gaiety, his wit, his complete lack of ostentation, his genuine goodness of heart broke down any inhibitions. He soon belonged and was made to feel that he belonged.

One element in this process was undoubtedly, after his ordination on 5 October, 1919, what may be termed the freemasonry of the Catholic priesthood. This is something difficult to convey to those who do not share it, but it is an

undeniable and powerful reality. Within the Church of God
there are, in addition to the great body of the secular clergy,
numerous religious orders, with their varying traditions and
individual characteristics. But, for all the superficial differences and disagreements which are often more present to the
consciousness of the laity than they are to the minds of those
who are supposed to be responsible for them, no priest, whatever his background or personal qualities, ever fails to realize
that these are insignificant when seen in the light of the grace
of ordination. This is the deep centre of his life; and at that
centre he meets and welcomes all his fellow priests.

So Ronald Knox, who all his life long never lost sight of or
failed to live up to realities of his priestly calling, kept this
special place in his heart for St. Edmund's, where he first
received that gift and where he first encountered, in an intimate way, his fellow priests. And they, in their turn, took him
to their hearts, not just because he was a good companion, but
because, shedding lustre on the priesthood, he made them
prouder still to be his fellows. But the debt was by no means
all one one side. Because it was in a group of priests that
Ronald spent the first formative years of his priesthood and
his Catholic life, this meant that he saw his Catholicism in
terms of the priesthood, and a priesthood with long memories
of ostracism and persecution. Thirty years later, when he
wrote *Let Dons Delight,* he made it clear that his sympathies
lay, not with the common-rooms, for all his enjoyment of
them, but with those who had been compelled for conscience'
sake to surrender the delights of Oxford life. He expressed a
profound personal conviction in a typical antithesis: "I was
taught where, we are assured on good authority, the battle of
Waterloo was won; I am teaching where the battle of
Tyburn was won; and I thank God for it."

It may well be true, as Mr. Waugh has said, that some of Ronald's friends regarded the years he spent at St. Edmund's "as a time of exile from his proper field." It is not quite certain that he would necessarily have agreed with those friends, nor was it then clear what his "proper field" was.

Certainly, it would seem, he did not feel that his next appointment, as chaplain to the Catholic undergraduates at Oxford, was particularly successful. On the face of it, of course, it was the obvious job for him, and his selection for it affords another example of the anxiety of his superiors to find for him the sort of position in which his talents might best be employed and in which he himself would be most likely to find satisfaction. Of course he was glad to be back at Oxford, though an Oxford sadly changed from the university to which, precisely twenty years before, he had first come up.

In the first place, it was haunted for him by ghosts, the ghosts of those many friends who had been taken from him in the War. Again, the Oxford he had known was the Oxford of his crusading Anglicanism; and now, separated from his former colleagues by his conversion, he was sadly aware—as the last chapter of *Let Dons Delight* makes clear—of the growing secularization of what had once represented the ideal of godliness and good learning. True, he found that some of his old friends, especially at Trinity, and at one or two other colleges in which his Balliol contemporaries now held fellowships, welcomed him back with enthusiasm; and in the Catholic community he was received with joy. Campion Hall took the place of Pusey House, especially after its migration to Brewer Street, when he and Father D'Arcy became next-door neighbours. (He once remarked that the thing that would make him happy would be to go for a walk with Fr. D'Arcy every afternoon.)

But he was no longer fully at ease with the undergraduates who were his special charge. They themselves were not always aware of this. They called him "Ronnie"—though more behind his back than to his face. They delighted in his company, they flocked to his talks and sermons—as they were to continue to flock to the very end of his active days; they felt proud of their chaplain, though, to be sure, they did not always find it easy to treat him simply as their chaplain.

Superficially, indeed, it was a very happy time for him. His reputation as a preacher was steadily growing; more and more he was coming to be accepted as the ablest Catholic apologist of the day; his circle of friends within the Church was increasing, and during the vacations he was able to get away from Oxford and stay in their houses.

But during the thirteen years—from 1926 to 1939—when he held this position, he was haunted by a melancholy sense of inadequacy. For the first time in his life, he had direct and permanent responsibility for the spiritual welfare of a group of young men at what is notoriously the most difficult and challenging period of their lives. Miserably aware of their failures, he attributed these to some lack in himself. He tried everything he could think of to interest, attract and encourage the young men in fidelity to their religion. But, having done all that was required of him, he still felt an unprofitable servant. Their relatively infrequent lapses were patent and, as he felt, a reflection on his guidance. Success in this department was supremely important; it was the only kind of success that seemed to elude him.

This kind of suffering was both a consequence of, and also a means of deepening, his great spiritual sensitivity. This was the true purgation he endured, not the relatively insignificant disappointments concerning one or two not tremendously important undertakings—the revision of the *Manual of Prayers* and the *Westminster Hymnal*—which have given rise to the legend that the Church did not make the fullest use of his talents. As against those, he could set any number of triumphs. The one success that really mattered seemed to be denied him. If he felt some degree of resentment at the way he was treated, on occasion, by others, he was still able to laugh at himself; you cannot laugh when the spiritual welfare, perhaps the eternal salvation, of your charges is at stake.

Nor was he able to appreciate the solid positive achievement to be set on the other side of the balance-sheet. First of all, he put the Oxford chaplaincy on the map—partly, indeed, because the number of Catholic undergraduates was growing steadily during the inter-war years, but still more because of his own personal contribution. Those who tended to think of him as a rather abstracted, unpractical type were surprised at the vigour and effective planning which he brought to bear on the many-sided problems of his new charge. He had inherited a building, of which the official title was the Old Palace; but the adjective was more true to the facts than the noun. Old it was, and needed much attention, some of which he noted down in the document entitled "The Whole Art of Chaplaincraft."

A personal and retrospective commentary on his own work may be found in the sermon which he preached on the occasion of the opening of the new chapel, the "rococo tin tabernacle," as he described it, which had been built by Mgr. Elwes to accommodate the inflated Catholic undergraduate population—perhaps double the size of that which Ronald had had in his care. The increase resulted from Government policy, embodied in the Education Act of 1944, providing greatly increased grants to enable a wider selection of undergraduates to aspire to university education. The sermon calls for quotation, not simply to illustrate the immediate point, but as an example of the way in which Ronald could combine, with a gentle mockery of his own tastes and the tastes of others, an abiding lesson concerning the really important things.

I cannot pretend that when I myself was chaplain here, the Old Palace was suspected of any exaggerated sympathy with the ardours, the illusions of Youth. It stood here, a gaunt reminder of the past, calculated to chill the aspirations of the visitor, to snub the half-baked modernism of his outlook . . . An old place, where the aesthete of the late twenties must expect to find an atmosphere of cheerful Philistinism flourishing unreproved; representational art, and bookshelves guiltless of modern poetry; if you wanted to hear about that sort of thing, you went round to Campion. An old place, where the near-Left political language of the early·thirties found no conspicuous echo; you could air progressive doctrines, but if you wanted to find a sympathetic hearing, you must look for it in Walton Well Road [where the Catholic Workers' College then stood]. Sixteen hundred and twenty-eight was inscribed legibly over the door-bell; you had the illusion, in those days, that time had stood still . . .

I used to think of the Old Chapel . . . as (in its way) a spiritual replica of the cenacle; a home of memories. After all, it was an Oratory for the Catholic undergraduates of Oxford; to be a son of the Catholic Church, to be an alumnus of Oxford, is to be hedged about with memories; it is an umbilical cord joining you to your past. And when we built the new chapel—what was then the new chapel—I wanted it to be in some sense a replica of the old. I did not mean it to be depressingly ecclesiastical. When Mr.

Arnold Crush, the architect, brought me a nice set of Gothic plans, I told him I was sorry, but I didn't want anything which couldn't be turned into tea-rooms later on . . .[15]

Needless to say, this is almost exactly what has happened. Ronald was to congratulate himself on his foresight when, under a later regime, the former chapel became a sort of club-room for the members of the Newman Society. Not, perhaps, that he would have altogether approved of the dart-board and the television set which form part of its present furnishing.

But it was not chiefly at the practical level that we must estimate Ronald's contribution to the Catholic cause in Oxford. When he came to the Old Palace, Catholicism was still very much an obscure and unappreciated force in the life of the university. True, Ronald's old friend Francis Urquhart was still bearing his gentle, unobtrusive witness to his faith; Francis de Zulueta, the first Catholic to hold a chair at Oxford since the Reformation, was esteemed alike for his scholarship and his personal integrity; and there were three or four other Catholics who were senior members of colleges. At Campion Hall, Father Martindale was still wielding great influence amongst the undergraduates; but he had never felt at home in senior common-rooms and was very soon to give up the academic life altogether for a wider apostolate. It was, then, still possible in effect to ignore the reality of the contribution made by Catholics to the life of the university.

When Ronald resigned his chaplaincy in 1939, a very different estimate would have to be made. It would be merely

[15] *The Occasional Sermons of Ronald A. Knox:* Edited, with an Introduction, by Philip Caraman, S.J., © Evelyn Waugh, 1960 (New York: Sheed and Ward, 1960), pp. 268-9.

silly to suggest that the change was brought about by his single-handed efforts. That would be to ignore the formidable contribution made by Father D'Arcy's personal charm and intellectual force; by the Dominicans at Blackfriars and the Benedictines at St. Benet's; by the steadily growing numbers of Catholic Fellows; by the unobtrusive work of Fr. O'Hea, who so zealously fostered the work initiated by Fr. Charles Plater. But these all had to make their way, whereas, despite the somewhat ambivalent attitude which official Oxford displayed towards one who had first dazzled it as an Anglican and then returned as a Catholic, Ronald Knox could hardly be regarded as an outsider. And, as never before, Oxford was enabled

> To see wit, laughter and the Popish creed
> Cluster and sparkle in the name of Knox.

Although, as we have already seen, the Oxford to which he returned as a Catholic was in many ways a different Oxford from the one he had left over ten years before, he himself saw it with a profounder insight. He saw it as originally cradled in the faith he now professed, he saw it as the erstwhile familiar home of those Benedictines and Dominicans and Franciscans who were now delighted to welcome him as a brother in the place to which they were now allowed to return; he saw it as the promised land which conscience had forbidden so many of the English Martyrs to enjoy. In a poignant passage from a sermon on the Oxford Martyrs we read these revealing words:

They were our fellow students; as they lay in prison, little vignettes of Oxford must have danced before them; the Cottages at Worcester, and Mob Quad at Merton, and Christ Church Hall, and Magdalen Tower, and New College cloisters, and the old library at Trinity and the front of St. John's, were as familiar sights to them as to us who follow them; they must remember them still, if heaven is to be the completion of our life on earth.[16]

In the course of a review Mr. Angus Wilson says:

There are times when Mr. Waugh seems to suggest that Knox was temperamentally depressive. I remember the only glimpses of him, an isolated figure walking around Christ Church Meadow on cheerless, leaf-strewn, windy October afternoons, and I can believe it.[17]

Yet the man who thus walked round the Meadow may well have been far from melancholy, as he saw himself the heir of the original Oxford, the Oxford which had disinherited, not him and his fellows, but herself. He may, indeed, have been wondering how best he could reinforce to his undergraduates the lesson of Oxford's authentic history; he may have been reflecting on the sadder aspects of present-day Oxford; but he may well have been remembering that

. . . not all the philosophies of Oxford are philosophies of negation and despair; she is fed by secret streams, not less influential to her life or less native to her genius.[18]

But what was almost certainly his greatest achievement was one which, in the nature of things, he could not himself realize. This is the lasting impression he made on the four generations of Catholic undergraduates who passed through his

---

[16] *Occasional Sermons*, p. 131.
[17] *Encounter* (January 1960).
[18] *The Hidden Stream* (New York: Sheed and Ward, 1953), p. vi.

hands. It was not the sort of thing they could tell him; many of them, doubtless, were hardly aware of it themselves at the time; some of them may have been hardly conscious of what he had done for them. Yet those who have come across these same undergraduates in later years have heard many a tribute paid to his teaching and to his influence.

By the kindness of Mr. Robert Speaight it is possible to quote one such example.

My brother Hugh came up to Oxford in 1927 . . . He had been received into the Church at Haileybury—well, not *at* Haileybury, because that's not the kind of thing that goes on at Haileybury—but while he was at the school. He thought he had a vocation to the Dominicans, but then he went though an odd psychological phase. The only person who could really have explained it to me was Eric Strauss, who knew him very well—understood and admired him—and now it is too late for me to ask him. Anyway, Hugh was a very troublesome subject to R.A.K., and when it came to inviting Alistair Crowley down to Oxford to speak, there was a stand-up row. Hugh's Dominican vocation evaporated, and after leaving Oxford he went on the *Morning Post* and in 1932 was appointed to their Paris office. Then he was suddenly hit with T.B., bore a long illness with incredible patience and courage, and in 1934 came home to die. I was then playing out at Streatham, and on the evening before his death I came back about midnight. Seeing the light still on in his room, I went in to say Goodnight to him. He was leaning back on his pillows, breathing with difficulty. He had been anointed a few days before. He then started talking about a novel he had written during his illness, an amusing and, I daresay, slightly outrageous affair called *The Prime Minister's Ear*. He gave me instructions about it—and then added. "By the way, if anything should happen with this, will you see that page so-and-so is suppressed, because I think it might give offence to Ronnie Knox." He died the following afternoon, and I wrote and told Ronnie about what were practically his last words; and Ronnie was deeply moved. I doubt if Hugh had seen Ronnie since he had left Oxford—he had cut quite adrift from his Oxford moorings and had become a very different person, though still an odd one. And this seemed to me an extraordinary example of Ronald's retrospective influence.[19]

"Retrospective influence" is an allusion to an appreciation of Ronald by one of the undergraduates who lodged with him at the Old Palace, Mr. David Walker. His appreciation concludes with the expressive words, "We gave him damn-all; he gave us a lot."[20]

Yet, conscious as he was that his duties as chaplain made it all but impossible to fulfil himself as a writer in the way he would have preferred, it is not unlikely that, given the scrupulosity of his conscience, he would have gone on to the end shouldering that burden, had it not been for what we cannot fail to see as a providential interposition.

[19] From a private letter.
[20] Waugh, *op. cit.*, p. 226.

2

HARVEST

WHEN RONALD KNOX handed over the chaplaincy to Father Alfonso de Zulueta in 1939, he was already in his fifty-second year. He was to end his life before his seventieth year was completed. Into these eighteen years he was to concentrate what must, by any standards, be regarded as his most important literary output. He had already spent almost exactly twenty years as a priest. Are we, then, to regard these twenty years as largely wasted, as a period during which his literary talents were, perforce, frustrated? The answer is undoubtedly that the very fertility and richness of his achievement in this time of harvesting was due to the long period during which his spiritual perceptiveness was developing in such a way as to add almost a new dimension to his preaching and writing. In his earlier period there was not lacking brilliance of artistic structure, subtlety of argument, aptness of literary or historical allusion, vividness of illustrative imagery—all the qualities which he possessed until the very end. But the characteristic warmth of human sympathy and depth of understanding seem to be more marked in these later years, to a degree far beyond anything he had achieved before his fiftieth year.

His sermons were always a joy to listen to; were they always such an inspiration as they later became? Put it another way: his earliest work appeals primarily to the head; it is expository, apologetic, scholarly. His latest work appeals more directly to the heart, not in any sentimental or purely "devotional" way—if anything, his earlier work was marked more by these features—but by some power of immediate appeal, some directness of human contact. The word has become a cliché, but no description seems so apt as the statement that he had mellowed.

The long process by which this came about culminated in almost dramatic fashion in the story of his friendship with Lady Acton. It is possible to exaggerate the importance of this incident. After his reception into the Church and his ordination to the priesthood, he had developed and was to develop a number of great friendships with women, conspicuous among them Lady Lovat and Mrs. Katherine Asquith, but there seems to have been a special quality about his relationship with Lady Acton. Invited, in 1937, to instruct her in the Faith with a view to her becoming a Catholic, he found in her at once a most apt pupil and a frank and outspoken critic. It may well be that, at a time when he was becoming increasingly affected by a sense of failure with the undergraduates entrusted to his care, his manifest success with this neophyte restored something of his self-confidence. Whatever the reason, he found, after twenty years, something of the perfection of companionship which he had lost when Guy Lawrence died.

The fact that she was remarkably attractive whilst he was now approaching his fiftieth year might so easily have become a source of spiritual trouble to him and of embarrassment to her. In effect what they achieved was one of those rare friendships between a man and a woman in which warmth of affection exists side by side with complete self-control and an absence of unhealthy emotionalism. Her marriage and her growing family, his vocation and his absorption in the task of translating the Bible, helped by the integrity and fastidiousness which both possessed, enabled them to develop and foster a relationship which brought to both of them great human happiness and a fulfilment both intellectual and spiritual. There can be no sort of doubt that for Ronald it came at a time when, for the reasons suggested above as well as because of various indispositions, he seemed to be coming to the end of his physical resources.

Yet he still felt that, if only he could get away from the demands of life in Oxford, he could produce work of lasting importance. For some years now he had been collecting material for the book which was eventually to become *Enthusiasm*. Under the impetus of Lady Acton's encouragement, he wrote in 1938 the book which was, by universal consent, one of his most perfect achievements—*Let Dons Delight*. With his intense concern for literary excellence coupled with his lifelong devotion to the Bible, he was eager to try his hand at a translation which might make that book a source of help and inspiration to the English Catholic public.

At Lady Acton's invitation, he decided that he would leave Oxford to become private chaplain at Aldenham Park, the Shropshire home of the Acton family. Leaving Oxford was, of course, a matter for the Hierarchy's decision; and when he mooted the suggestion to Cardinal Hinsley, the effect was that the latter proposed that he should become President of St. Edmund's. This was not quite what he was hoping for, but with characteristic conscientiousness he consulted his confessor, Fr. Justin McCann, the Master of St. Benet's Hall, and Father D'Arcy, who not only knew Ronald well but could also estimate the contribution which he could make in the proposed position. Both agreed that he ought not to accept, and he wrote at great length to the Cardinal to state his views.

Once again, he received a letter full of delicate understanding, expressing complete readiness to facilitate his plans for doing some writing. In the course of the letter occurs this sentence, which may be taken as summing up the attitude of mind, not only of Cardinal Hinsley himself, but of all who were, at any time, responsible for Ronald's work: "Your interest and wishes are decisive; I bow submissively." As a priest, he was under obedience to his bishop; he was treated with a special appreciation of his gifts, and there was a complete absence of that ruthless insistence which is so freely attributed to ecclesiastical authority by those who have little experience of it. In July 1939, he took up his abode at Aldenham.

Before this move to Aldenham had taken place, the affair of the *Manual of Prayers* had occurred. Ronald was asked by the Hierarchy to undertake a new version of their official collection of prayers. He appears to have done his work with a thoroughness which alarmed some bishops, and, in the end, his extensive alterations were not accepted. Doubtless he was disappointed that his work did not win acceptance; doubtless there was some misunderstanding on both sides as to the precise terms of his commission; possibly there was some carelessness, tactlessness and lack of consideration in the way the withdrawal was handled. But that he had in no way forfeited the confidence of the Hierarchy is shown by the fact that he was so soon to be commissioned by them to undertake the much more important task of translating the Bible.

Nor, on his side, did the incident affect his attitude to them or to the Catholic body as a whole. Naturally, during the war years his opportunities for travel became few—to say nothing of the increasing demands made on him by his translation. But, with the return of peace, invitations to preach came crowding in and were not refused, unless some urgent reason compelled a refusal. The reason was never one of personal preference, still less of personal pique.

One occasion lives in the memory. In 1954, when Archbishop Grimshaw was enthroned at Birmingham, Ronald was invited to preach in the Cathedral of St. Chad's. No one who was then present is likely to forget what a triumphant occasion this was for the preacher. Not only was the sermon itself a superb example of his art, combining wit and humour with profound spirituality and aptness of teaching; the obvious pride and affection manifested by the large assembly of bishops and other clerical notabilities filled him with manifest satisfaction and happiness. No one who witnessed that scene could ever subscribe to the view that Ronald ever felt himself at odds with his brethren.

Meanwhile, of course, the great work of his life, the work which was made possible only by the generous understanding of his superiors, had been completed. Single-handed, in a space of little over ten years, he had produced the translation of the Bible, which must ever remain his great monument. It was, incidentally, an achievement which demanded both a rigid discipline and a high degree of composure. It was carried through in circumstances which might well have frayed the nerves of anyone not blessed with a robust temperament. The idyllic picture which, in anticipation, doubtless presented itself to Ronald's imagination—a life of peace and ample leisure, in a comfortable home with congenial companionship—was soon shattered. Shortly after he had settled down with his books and typewriter, war descended upon the world and an army of schoolgirls and nuns descended upon Aldenham. The Community of the Assumption, evacuated from their London home in Kensington Square, were to spend the next seven years as an unexpected addition to the household.

This meant, in effect, that the greater part of the house was denied to Lady Acton and to Ronald, and finally he was confined to one room, which not only housed all his books—commentaries, lexicons, the entire set of the Oxford English Dictionary, and all the necessary apparatus of the scholar—but was also used by Lady Acton as her own writing-room, as well as their common dining-room. Here, after breakfast, he would settle down to a morning's work. The afternoon was usually spent in some form of exercise—walking, bathing in summer, or working on the land. After tea would follow another spell of translation, but, as a rule, little work was done after dinner.

To help Ronald with their advice and comments, a committee, representing the Hierarchy and the different religious orders, had been appointed by their various superiors. We know that Ronald and Father Martindale, to Ronald's great distress, failed to see eye to eye on principles of translation, and Ronald used whimsically to tell how, one day, he spoke to one of the nuns about his difficulties. The nun duly promised her prayers, with the "result" that Father Martindale went to Denmark, where he was interned for the rest of the war. In his place the Provincial appointed another member of the Society, who has never ceased to be grateful for the opportunity thus afforded him of establishing close relations with Ronald.

It was originally intended that the committee of advisers should meet at regular intervals, but the difficulties of wartime travel ruled this out, and after the first year the committee met only once, under the chairmanship of the Bishop of Lancaster. Contact was maintained by post, Ronald sending round a copy of each Gospel or Epistle as he finished it, asking for comments, to which he faithfully replied, sometimes accepting suggestions, more often pointing out why suggestions had already been considered by him and rejected for reasons stated.

It is not without mild interest that, as one of the committee lived at Maynooth, which was in a neutral country, it was necessary to send the various manuscripts to him through the censor at Liverpool. It was with some amusement that we thought of that official solemnly reading through a translation of the New Testament, in case information should somehow be being passed to the enemy.

To stay at Aldenham with Ronnie and watch him at work was a chastening and inspiring experience. The meticulous care with which the text was studied, the reference to half a dozen authorities about some disputed passage, the scrupulous investigation of Murray's dictionary to see how old a usage might be—all this was both impressive and reassuring. It gave the lie to any suggestion that here was a translation thrown off almost casually. The wonder is that, granted all the difficulties under which he was working and the precision of method employed, he was able to finish the huge task in such a comparatively short time.

Whilst one could sympathize with him over the manifest obstacles that beset his path, there can be no sort of doubt that he was, for all his superficial grumbles, profoundly happy. There was, of course, the help and inspiration of Lady Acton herself, immersed though she was in running the estate in her husband's absence and in bringing up, with a minimum of help, her growing family; surprisingly too, the presence of the schoolgirls, far from being the nuisance it might well have been, provided yet another outlet for his adaptable genius in the regular sermons which he gave them. It also gave him new friends, who showed him the simple affection of the young and some of whom were to grow up to be very close to his heart.

But above all it was his translation that brought him the richest satisfaction. There were times, inevitably, when the sheer labour of the task oppressed him a little; when the criticisms of the conservative diehard irritated him; when he grew apprehensively despondent about the prospects of success. None of this ever affected his output or his assiduity. Calmly, patiently, inexorably he went on, doing his daily stint, never relaxing his vigilance or losing sight of his goal—the production of a Bible which would be accurate, idiomatic, intelligible.

This is not the place for an estimate of the translation as a literary achievement, but perhaps a word or two more may be said about it as a human achievement. Clearly it has its defects, as the original Bible has its defects, judged by the highest literary standards. No translation of any work is ever going to be universally acceptable. The Bible, in particular, with all its associations and overtones, has come to take on a quality of sacredness which has nothing to do directly with its specifically religious content. (Faced with a certain type of

criticism, Ronald would complain that people seemed much
more concerned with what the Bible sounded like than with
what it meant.)

What he was trying to do, and what to a very great extent
he did, was to bring out the meaning of the Scriptures. It is
universally admitted that he succeeded superbly with St.
Paul's Epistles. But his success was considerable even with the
Old Testament, not least with the Sapiential books, the
Prophets and the Psalms.

Even if it had not been as good as it is, the work would
have been remarkable, simply as a *tour de force*. To have
succeeded in a space of ten years in translating the Bible with
accuracy, intelligibility and due reverence is a feat that few
men could have carried through single-handed. His committee of advisers may have helped on individual points, as he
frankly recognized in his preface to the first edition of the
New Testament:

Their criticisms throughout have been of the utmost value, and
have had a greater influence on the present form of the text
than they themselves can be induced to realise.

But inevitably they added to his labours, since their animad-
versions had to be studied, copied out, circulated, discussed,
answered or incorporated into his text.

In addition, as we have seen, there were the distractions and
vexations of wartime life at Aldenham, the virtual absence
of help with the purely physical tasks of typing, tying up
parcels, circulating manuscripts and all the time-wasting trivialities which he could never delegate, largely out of that great
humility of his, which could not see why he should demand

such services of other people. (He used to say, with that characteristic wry humour, that his favourite mortification was letting other people do things for him.)

It is easy to say that all this was a great waste of his time. In one sense it was. Yet, given what he was, it was all inevitable. And it is precisely because he was what he was that he was able to have on others the tremendous influence he did exert. It was because, despite Eton, despite Balliol, he preserved the feeling of being an ordinary sort of person, that he could so vividly appeal to the ordinary person. His greatness lay in the fact that he could take for granted his extraordinary gifts of intelligence and sensitivity, of linguistic ability and psychological insight, seeing himself always as not out of the ordinary. Self-importance is an indication of small-mindedness. He was too large-minded, too large-hearted not to think that other people were just as important as, nay more important than, himself.

This was why his volumes of commentary on the New Testament, companion pieces to his translation, were so successful. For all his scholarship, he could appreciate the problems which the ordinary reader of the Gospels or of St. Paul was likely to feel. It is the very simplicity, in a way, the very obviousness, of his suggestions which makes them so effective. How refreshingly unlike so much "Johannine" scholarship is the following:

Once the Fourth Gospel is treated as a problem it becomes an insoluble problem . . . It seems to be the reminiscences of a very old man, who has an old man's tricks of narration. He will recall, as if conjuring them up with difficulty, details about names and places and relationships which have nothing much to do with the story. He will give us little footnotes, as if to make sure that we are following; often unnecessary, often delayed instead of being put in their proper place. He will remember fragments of a conversation, passing on from this utterance to that by mere association of memory, instead of giving us a reasoned précis of the whole. He will alternately assume that we know the story already, and narrate it in meticulous detail. He will pass from one scene to another without giving us warning of the change.[1]

It is important, then, in considering the translation, to bear in mind what he was at. He had no desire to compete with any existing version, to reproduce the sonorous cadences of the Authorised Version, the archaisms of Douai, the up-to-the-minute renderings of Moffat or Phillips. His primary purpose, probably his sole purpose, was to make the word of God as intelligible in the twentieth century as it had been in the first. It would have been easy for the author of *Let Dons Delight* to produce a pastiche of Lucan or Johannine or Pauline writing; but this would have been merely to introduce another distraction. As far as possible he wanted to do away with distractions, to produce that limpidity of style which does not come between the reader and the subject-matter. If those who read his translation were plagued by familiar echoes, that was a pity; but it was no concern of his.

If there were misgivings in some minds during the early stages of the work, there can be no sort of doubt that the official welcome accorded to the finished text of the New Testament was as warm-hearted as it was enthusiastic.

[1] *A Commentary on the Gospels* (New York: Sheed and Ward, 1952), pp. xv-xvi.

In commissioning Mgr. Knox to undertake this great work, the Hierarchy knew well his rich academic attainments. Their choice has been fully justified, for his masterly command of English language and limpid style have combined to produce the lucid text now before us.

Time alone will reveal the full merits of this translation. For the moment it can be said that there is an engaging freshness about the narrative which captivates the reader, and a clarity of expression which removes the obscurity of not a few passages in former translations.

This tribute from Cardinal Griffin evoked a delighted response from Ronald. Significantly, the Cardinal had sent Ronald a copy of his proposed preface, and this is the expression of gratitude which it elicited.

I don't think that, in any of the day-dreams I have indulged these last five and a half years, I envisaged the possibility of bringing out the New Testament with such a generous tribute from authority prefaced to it. I would not want a word of it altered and I don't know how to thank you for giving me such a splendid send-off.

Those who are determined to believe that the Hierarchy is a body of narrow-minded bigots who are reluctant to tolerate any activity which they do not rigidly control will doubtless retort that, having done their best to frustrate Ronald's ambitions, they now changed their tactics, because they saw a lucrative proposition in the new translation. After all, the copyright was invested in them. It would be foolish not to boost the work.

Whilst it is true that, by the standards of literary men with abilities comparable to Ronald's, the £200 a year paid to him by the Hierarchy must seem paltry, the fact remains that he was—and knew himself to be—first and foremost a priest. He realized that few priests in the country were receiving from their superiors anything like that allowance, for work which, naturally speaking, was far less congenial. He had been officially "commissioned" to do the translation; but it was a work he was himself desperately anxious to perform. Having no parochial duties, he was free to accept many an engagement which would constitute a significant increase in his income. He was, in theory, free to do as much or as little work on translation in any given period of time as he saw fit.

In fact, as we know, by his own request the payment was discontinued in 1950—most of it was going to the Treasury in income tax—and when it had been suggested that he should have a share in the royalties, he declined this offer in words which must go on record.

I hope it doesn't seem horribly priggish, but I have developed a very strong scruple against cashing in, as a private person, on the word of God. So if you don't mind, my idea is to make Watt [his agent] pay in all royalties to you [the Hierarchy].

In any case, those who were sufficiently close to Ronald suspected, though he tried to hide, how much money he gave away in charity. Mr. Chambers asserts that "he probably *gave* in twenty years £10,000 to £15,000 to the Converts' Aid Society . . . For considerably more than thirty years he had spoken and preached for us in various parts of England, Scotland and Wales . . . Preacher's fees and travelling expenses were subjects that dared not be mentioned!"

Whatever sum he accepted from the Hierarchy, therefore, was likely to go in charity anyway. Nor was he the sort of person who needed to have his personal vanity flattered by feeling that he could "command" large sums in fees. In his personal habits he was frugal to the point of discomfort—the result, doubtless, of a combination of causes. Early experience of the need for economy was reinforced by an ascetic discipline which bordered at times on the puritanical. With that self-depreciatory manner which enabled him to disguise his austerities under a mask of mockery, he accused himself of being "stingy."

A trivial incident may serve as an illustration. Staying with him on one occasion, a guest, in the course of discussing overnight the timing of their use of the bathroom next morning, asked him how long it took him to shave. With that well-known combination of slight bashfulness, mock seriousness and down-to-earth practicality, he said, "Well, it's nearing Quarter Day, so it's taking me a bit longer at present." In answer to the lifted eyebrow came the answer: "You see, I put in a new blade every Quarter Day . . ."

Towards the end of his life, on an occasion when he was being seen off at Oxford, he remarked: "I've made a curious New Year resolution—always to travel first" (i.e., in a "first-class" rather than a "second-class" compartment) the reason being, not that this would enable him to travel in greater comfort, but because he would be able to work better. For, whilst it is true that he always had leisure for his guests, and seemed to spend a not inconsiderable amount of time over his Patience, doing *The Times* crossword puzzle, and playing games like Scrabble with great assiduity, he was not a man to waste time. His recreations were almost literally what the

term suggests, activities which restored his intellectual ener-
gies. His private detective, Bredon, as we know, used to solve
his problems over a complicated form of Patience. There was
surely something autobiographical about this touch. Much of
his life can be understood only by those who realize how
much he had taken to heart St. Ignatius's fundamental principle about the proper use of creatures.

The thing which comes first is your job. You are not a statue
standing on a pillar, you are a cog in a machine. And when I talk
about your job, I don't mean simply the means by which you
earn your bread, or the work which you do directly for the
glory of God. I mean all the complex of social relations which
make up your life. It is part of your job to be kind to other
people, not to squash them, to cheer them up, not to depress
them. The kind of self-denial God certainly does ask of you is
the kind of self-denial that will make you more useful to your
fellow-men. And the kind of self-denial he certainly does not ask
of you is the kind of self-denial which will turn you into a prig
or a wet-blanket or a nervous wreck . . . You mustn't try to force
your nature into a wholly different pattern; you must be what
God made you, only trying to make of it what God meant you
to make of it. Your hand always lying light on the tiller, ready to
catch any breath of guidance that God will send you.[2]

So much, indeed, had he taken it to heart that it became
something almost of second nature in him to examine his conscience about his attitude to creatures, above all to creature
comforts. He was not morbidly introspective; but he, who
had such clarity of vision about human nature and its weaknesses, was not blind to the temptations to which he might

[2] *Retreat for Lay People* (New York: Sheed and Ward, 1955), pp. 199-200.

succumb. There is a revealing passage in a sermon on Edmund Campion which, in one place, asks:

Why did Campion turn Jesuit? It is the least explained incident in his career. There were English Jesuits already, but they were few; it was Campion who set the fashion. If we did not know our man, we might have suspected him of running away from danger; Douai was the road to martyrdom, and it looked for a time as if he would end his days teaching at Prague. My suspicion is that at Douai they made too much of him, hailed him as a great intellect; he might be left there to write controversial treatises, be turned on, perhaps, to translate the Bible . . .[3]

The words were written when he had just finished translating the Bible himself, and had not a few controversial works to his credit. He cannot have failed to mark the parallel. If he did not join the Society to escape the dangers of being made too much of, he certainly took every means to ensure that he did not succumb to such dangers. He saw his talents as God-given tools, not to be employed as profitmaking abilities. Of him it might be said, as he himself, in that same sermon, said of Campion:

There was a great simplicity about his mind, for all his uncommon powers of reasoning.

It has become a commonplace to compare Ronald Knox with Newman. In some ways the comparison is inevitable. But there is a truer parallel between him and another famous Oxford convert, a Balliol man like himself, the poet Gerard Manley Hopkins. Of Hopkins, too, it has been said that, by

[3] *Occasional Sermons*, p. 139.

becoming a priest, above all a Jesuit, he wasted his life, his talents were frustrated, he never fulfilled his early promise. Yet it seems at least arguable, on the evidence, that, had he not become a Jesuit, he would have become an ineffective dilettante, morbidly obsessed with his personal problems, writing pretty poems of a somewhat sentimental kind, but having little permanent influence.

When he was uncertain about his vocation, Newman wrote to Hopkins, "Do not call the Jesuit discipline hard; it will bring you to Heaven." It did something else. The resolution he formed on entering the Jesuit novitiate to make a complete sacrifice of his poetic gifts meant that when, in due course, he resumed the writing of poetry, he came to his task with a mind richly stored with all the experience of ten years' meditation on the profound truths of the Christian faith as distilled through the exercises of St. Ignatius. The great work on which his reputation was founded—*The Wreck of the Deutschland*—was the direct outcome of his experiences as a Jesuit.

Moreover, the story of his career as a priest, to those who study it with care, shows how much his Superiors sought to find the right outlet for his special abilities. If none of his various postings brought him happiness, if the later years of his life were clouded with spiritual anguish, due to a complication of causes, none of this should be laid at the door of uncomprehending or ruthless superiors.

By contrast, of course, Ronald's life was a triumphant success, but the success was undeniably due precisely to the discipline into which he entered. Had he remained an Anglican, he might well have had a more spectacular and superficially brilliant career; but he might well have dissipated his talents in the relative trivialities of Tractarian polemics. As Hopkins needed the stiffening of Jesuit asceticism, so the fixed authority of the Catholic Church and the traditional austerities of its priesthood afforded Ronald the well-defined framework within which he could most fully deploy his talents.

Had he remained an Anglican, could he have written anything remotely like the following passage from *The Belief of Catholics?*

Where you see men, in the old world or in the new, full of the conviction that there is one visible Church, and that separation from it is spiritual death; where you see men, in the old world or in the new, determined to preserve intact those traditions of truth which they have received from their forefathers, and suspicious of any theological statement which has even the appearance of whittling them away; where you see men distrustful of the age they live in, knowing that change has a Siren voice, and the latest song is ever the most readily sung; where you see men ready to hail God's Power in miracle, to bow before mysteries which they cannot explain, and to view this world as a very little thing in comparison with eternity; where you see men living by the very high standards of Christian ambition, yet infinitely patient with the shortcomings of those who fall below it—there you have the Catholic type.[4]

Words such as these, clearly echoing the cadences of Newman, yet from a deep inner conviction, remind us that Ronald Knox was first and foremost a Catholic and can be judged only from that standpoint. It is thus he would have wished to be judged. The achievement of which he would have been most proud was the achievement of shedding lustre

[4] New Edition (New York: Sheed and Ward, 1953), p. 143.

on the Catholic faith which was his dearest prize and greatest boast.

Before he had completed his work of translating the Bible, one more uprooting occurred—the last in his life. Lord Acton, buying a property in Rhodesia with the intention of emigrating there, left in February 1947, to be followed later by the rest of his family. Ronald was homeless. In October of that same year, having said Mass for the last time in the chapel in which, year after year, he had preached his *Slow Motion* sermons, he transferred his library and the rest of his effects to Mells. Here, for the last ten years of his life, he found the peace which undergraduates had denied to him at Oxford, schoolchildren at Aldenham.

In a curiously fitting way, the threads of his life were drawing together in a final pattern. One of his earliest school friends, at Summer Fields, at Eton and on to Balliol, had been Edward Horner, son of Lady Horner. The lovely Manor House, close by the glorious tower of Mells church, had been in the Horner family since the Dissolution of the Monasteries in the sixteenth century. Mellowed by time, the house had been adorned not least by the devoted care and artistic sensibility of Edward's mother. And now it was Edward's sister, Mrs. Katherine Asquith, who presided over and preserved all the beauty she had inherited.

The war which had robbed Ronald of so many of his friends, including Edward Horner, had robbed Edward's sister of her husband, the brilliant Raymond Asquith, son of the Liberal Prime Minister. She had become a Catholic after his death, and her eldest daughter, Helen, had been received into the Church by Ronald himself. Her son, Julian, a Balliol scholar like Ronald, had lodged at the Old Palace during his last year at Oxford. Ronald, therefore, had long-enduring links with the family and was familiar with the House. It was not inappropriate that he should join the family to act as chaplain, not merely to them but to the small Catholic community scattered about the neighbourhood. Helen's sister, Perdita, who had also become a Catholic, lived only three miles away at Ammerdown Park, with her three children. In the village lived Mr. and Mrs. Christopher Hollis with their four children.

Apart from his not infrequent short absences necessitated by preaching engagements, broadcast talks, retreats and similar activities, Ronald rarely left Mells. But twice he went abroad—something that had never happened since 1937. The first journey, in 1953, was a short visit to an old friend stationed in Germany. The next year was to see him embarked on the most extensive tour he ever made. Mrs. Asquith's son, now in the Colonial Service, was *en poste* in Zanzibar, and she and Ronald went out at the beginning of February to visit him. On the way there, they stayed at Government House in Nairobi—a detail which suggested to Ronald that he should entitle the diary he was writing *Through Smartest Africa*. When they came to Zanzibar he experienced a slight disillusionment. "I heard so much about the cathedral at Zanzibar," he said later, "but when I got there I found it was just like St. Aloysius"—the Jesuit church in Oxford.

He himself went on alone to Rhodesia, to stay with the Actons. The occasion for his visit was the christening of the latest of the Acton children; but he would hardly have gone all that way just for that, had it not afforded an opportunity of seeing again the friend whom he had not met for nearly five years. Clearly the visit was a cause of great happiness, and when he came back to England he spoke of the whole enterprise with such manifest contentment that he had obviously found in it a great refreshment of spirit.

Even the mishap of failing to make a connection with the weekly plane from Dar-es-Salaam was mentioned by him as something of a joke. To one who treated Bradshaw's railway time-table as a work of supreme importance, whose journeys by train were planned with meticulous precision, who suffered confessedly from train-fever and would always insist on being at the station well ahead of the time advertised for the departure of the train, there was something almost Gargantuan in the idea of missing a plane by a whole week.

During the following year he received one of the most emphatic expressions of public appreciation. To signalize the publication of the Knox Bible in one volume, his publishers organized a luncheon, presided over by the Cardinal and attended by well over two hundred guests. They represented a remarkable cross-section of the Catholic body in this country, together with a few friends from his Anglican days. Representatives of both Houses of Parliament, professional men of many kinds, those who would claim no particular distinction —all were united in their eagerness to do honour to one whom they genuinely loved. The Hierarchy was strongly represented, as well as every rank of the clergy, both secular and regular.

Those who listened to the speeches of welcome, of praise, of affectionate appreciation, were delighted to share in the pleasure which the guest of honour felt in this unequivocal and universal recognition of his achievement and of his own personal qualities. No one, listening to his reply, could suspect that his life was to be cut short within less than two years. He was so obviously in the full enjoyment of his powers. Here were to be recognized still the gifts which had captivated the Union almost half a century before; the gifts which had stirred the hearts of listeners in churches and chapels for the last forty years; the gifts which had charmed his friends in common-room and drawing-room, in presbytery and calefactory, ever since he had entertained his family with his precocious wit.

Eloquence and erudition, the magical phrase, the warm humanity, the spiritual perceptiveness, the personal modesty —all this and so much more combined to make this one of the most effective of the countless speeches he had ever delivered. For all the size of the party, it seemed to be an intimate occasion, so compulsively did the personality of the speaker respond to the universal affection in which he was held. Had any stranger come upon that assembly, he would surely have said not, This is a great man, but rather, This is a man very widely and very dearly loved.

It is almost impossible for one who was present on that occasion to pick up the "Knox Bible" and not recall the whimsical modesty with which he had glanced at this title, conferred "not by my wish."

Such a phrase dazzles you for a moment with a hint of immortality; but a little reflection will convince you that there is no immortality about lending your name to a product. Become a household word, and you are speedily forgotten. What housewife ever wastes a thought on the memory of President Hoover? What traveller ever recalls the existence of George Mortimer Pullman? In what refreshment room will you find a portrait of the fourth Earl of Sandwich?

Who but Ronald would have bothered to look up the Christian names of Mr. Pullman? Who but he would have remembered that it was the *fourth* Earl of Sandwich whose ghost haunts the refreshment rooms of British Railways?

There is one further question in that same speech which may have passed almost unnoticed.

Probably there is no such thing as a satisfactory translation of the Holy Scriptures. How should mere cleverness catch their supernatural overtones?

"Mere cleverness"? No. A decent modesty is here passing over into Christian humility. For he did not approach the task of translating the Bible in the spirit in which he had, years before, produced a school edition of some books of the *Aeneid* or had collaborated in writing a pastiche of Horace. Into his translation of the Bible went, indeed, all his gifts of scholarship and his sense of language. But into it, too, went that sense of reverence for God's revelation and that awareness of the importance of spiritual values which led him to attempt a translation of the *Imitation of Christ* as an occupation to fill in the hours of train travelling or which inspired him, in the closing months of his illness, to keep going at an English rendering of *La Vie d'une Âme*—the autobiography of the Little Flower. It is a far cry from Balliol to Lisieux, and there would seem to be little in common between the author of *French with Tears* and the young Carmelite.

Indeed, with characteristic self-mockery, he pictured St. Thérèse as suggesting for the translator of her work "Ronald Knox—he'll mind my style so terribly"—but there was a deep affinity between his simple-minded approach to religion (simple-minded because single-minded, and despite all his "mere cleverness") and her own "little way."

It was, in fact, only when one had got to know him well enough to pierce the great wall of reserve behind which he hid so much of himself, and to talk about the supernatural realities, that one came to appreciate the genuine concern for sanctity which was the most real thing about him. Like the rest of us he had his superficial faults, his sensitiveness to criticism, his occasional testiness, what seemed like exaggerated reactions to the minor frustrations of life; in another man, they would hardly have been noticed. In him, they were surprising because one almost automatically judged him by the highest standards. But none of them mattered, or could in any way diminish the high respect and deep affection he commanded.

Certainly they could never cast a shadow on the recognition of his genuine goodness. At Mells, as at Aldenham, whilst he obviously welcomed and enjoyed the frequent visits of friends, his life revolved more and more round the two poles of his study and the chapel across the lawn. His morning Mass, meticulously and unhurriedly performed, was always preceded by the statutory period of mental prayer; his day's work was punctuated by the recitation of the Divine Office; he was scrupulous about everything that pertained to the Church's official worship of God. But all this was merely the outward expression of a reality that no man can judge. One could only sense that his treasure lay more and more in that heaven to which his whole life had invariably pointed.

So his last illness found him not unprepared. Somehow, although one never thought of Ronald as robust, he was equally not a man one associated with sickness. To visit him in

hospital was to experience a sense of shock, as at seeing someone out of his natural element. But to visit him at Mells, during those last months when his friends knew what he was
blessedly unaware of, was to grow in appreciation and under
standing of the inner strength drawn from a faith which had
always been tested, but never found wanting.

Apart from the support of his friends, the unfailing kindness of those who were closest to him—at the risk of seeming
forward, one must pay a special tribute to the delicate consideration and devoted patience shown to him by Mrs. Asquith and her daughter, Lady Helen—the greatest natural
encouragement he felt during these difficult months was the
invitation he had received to deliver the Romanes Lecture at
Oxford. It was, as he rather sadly declared, the first time the
university had done anything to show her appreciation of
him. Oxford has a way of taking her sons for granted, on the
whole being concerned to honour those who do not belong.
Happily she had made amends, just in time, and in exactly the
right way. An honorary degree is a gesture of recognition, an
academic honour conferred on those whose achievements
may well lie outside the academic field. To be invited to deliver the Romanes Lecture was to be associated with some of
the most distinguished names in the modern English scene
since Gladstone gave the first of the series in 1892.

The invitation had been received before the end of 1956,
when already the hand of death was beginning to cast its
shadow. An extensive operation, a spell in hospital and a
period of what he thought of as convalescence, all intervened
to prevent his beginning to write the lecture until the following March, within three months of the date of its delivery.
Despite sheer physical weakness, due partly to an almost com-

plete loss of appetite, and a growing general discomfort, he set to work then, determined as ever to maintain the highest standards.

We are not here concerned with the literary achievement, with a study of the technical quality of this, his last completed work. But it is relevant to study the lecture in all its circumstances for the light it casts upon the character and spiritual quality of its author. Who is to analyse with certainty the motives that enabled him to rise above the handicaps which, in many another, would have rendered impossible the production of anything worth while, let alone anything of such outstanding merit.

In the first place, we need not doubt, came the habit of mind which, from his early days, had made it impossible for him to be content with anything second-rate. Whatever the occasion, however uncritical the audience might be expected to show itself, he remained always his own sternest critic. Now he was faced with an audience which was likely to be amongst the most critical he had ever addressed. For college tutors, criticism becomes almost instinctive. Undergraduates, in their turn, can be the most devastating of judges. His friends would be there, sympathetic but expectant; least of all, would he wish to fail them.

The lecture itself, displaying all the familiar qualities of incisive comment, sensitive appreciation, illustrative parallel, wide-ranging knowledge, felicity of diction and all-pervasive humour, was manifestly the work of a man who had enjoyed writing it. The joy of the craftsman manipulating his tools and deploying his skill had sustained him, enabling him to bend his slender physical resources to serve the demands of his mind.

But sheer duty was there, too, the consciousness that he had accepted, in happier times, an obligation which he could not now deny without belying his whole tradition. This was a great occasion, to which he must rise, cost what it might. It is only the thin-minded who would ascribe this to some kind of personal vanity. Personal vanity is such a trivial thing that it would never have supported him through that period of grinding effort. Personal pride, yes; that deep urge of our natures which will not let us fall below our best, but can impel us, at times, to rise to unsuspected heights, the pride that meets a challenge with resolution to prevail.

Through all this, surely, the grace of God was at work, that grace which he had nourished throughout his life, in a spirit of dry faith, as he so often hints, without knowing how well he was succeeding.

It is such a tiny surface of our souls that really lies under our observation. When some friend indulges in self-analysis, how wrong they nearly always are! Even we can see it . . . "I am brought to nothing, I am all ignorance, standing there like a dumb beast before thee"; let us be content to say that, with King David, and leave our Lord to do what he wants with us, down there in the depths which are beyond our knowing.[5]

No, he did not know; nor can we know. But we can guess, and believe that, all these last weary months, as he waited for the end, which at first he did not suspect to be so imminent, but was soon to suspect and then to know, he was being prepared for the final reckoning. Through his fidelity to his allotted task, he was proving his fidelity to God.

[5] *The Layman and His Conscience,* © Evelyn Waugh, 1961 (New York: Sheed and Ward, 1962), p. 178.

On 11 June 1957, in the evening, a vast company assembled in the Sheldonian for what many knew to be his last public appearance. A table was prepared, so that he could read his lecture sitting down, not standing, as the custom was. Everything had been done to spare his limited store of physical energy. He was not even to enter in formal procession, escorted by bedel, led in by the Vice-Chancellor. So he slipped into his place, unostentatiously, as he would always have preferred. When he appeared, even those who had seen him quite lately at Mells were shocked to see the way in which the ravages of the diseased liver had stained his face an almost brilliant yellow, set off by the whiteness of the collar. The Vice-Chancellor entered. The lecture began.

We held our breath for the first paragraph, wondering if we should be disappointed—disappointed in the quality of the work, disappointed in the delivery, which might fail to do justice to the text. We need not have feared. The voice, gentle as ever, yet clear and strong, began. All the old magic was there. Ripple after ripple of laughter ran through the theatre, to be hushed to silence as his argument developed. Few knew, and those who did not know could hardly suspect, the nature of the difficulties under which he had laboured to produce this superb analysis of the task of the translator. The range of knowledge seemed inexhaustible, the precision of memory so astonishing, the penetration of judgement so accurate. It was a triumph of literary criticism; still more was it a triumph of simple human courage.

We almost forgot that he was under sentence of death, until the calm, serene voice quoted, as an example of exact and faithful translation, the almost too familiar rendering by William Johnson Cory of a Greek epigram:

They told me, Heraclitus, they told me you were dead;
They brought me bitter news to hear, and bitter tears to shed;
I wept as I remembered how often you and I
Had tired the sun with talking and sent him down the sky.
And now that thou art lying, my dear old Carian guest,
A handful of grey ashes, long, long ago at rest,
Still are thy pleasant voices, thy nightingales, awake;
For death he taketh all away, but them he cannot take.

Again we held our breath, this time in awed astonishment. Was this deliberate, a self-conscious piece of artistry, playing on our emotions for the sake of effect? Impossible, in the circumstances, that it was not; impossible, knowing the man, that it could be. Certainly, there was no break in the voice, no hint of overemphasis. Well as he knew that his Oxford friends, in all probability, would never see him there again, as he would never talk again with them into the far night, his restraint and reserve were always so marked that such a public leave-taking seemed wholly out of character. This was supreme artistry, indeed, but all the more effective for being unstudied. Only, we knew.

One other moment of that memorable occasion lives in the memory with special vividness. Describing how the translator "must, in fact, get inside somebody else's skin before he undertakes the rendering of a single sentence", he went on to quote from his own immediate experience.

I myself am committed at the moment to the autobiography of St. Theresa of Lisieux. It is not a simple process to put yourself inside the skin of a young . . . French . . . female . . . saint.[6]

[6] *Literary Distractions*, © Evelyn Waugh, 1958 (New York: Sheed and Ward, 1958), pp. 53-4.

The pauses between the last four words were emphatic and significant. "Here am I," he seemed to be saying, "an elderly Englishman, anything but a saint," trying to do the seemingly impossible.

But you have got, somehow, to sink your own personality and wrap yourself round in a mood whenever you sit down at your writing-table for such work as this. All translation is a kind of impersonation. . . .[7]

Oxford is not unacquainted with lecturers innumerable, from the routine faculty lecturers to distinguished and talented speakers of every kind. Audiences usually accord to those who have addressed them a meed of applause varying from the polite and perfunctory to the sustained and enthusiastic. There could be no doubt that this lecture and this lecturer commanded universal and delighted approval.

That evening, the Vice-Chancellor, who had issued the invitation to Ronald to deliver the lecture, had asked a few of the lecturer's closest friends to a small party in the Provost's lodgings at Worcester. It was out of the question to have even the most restricted dinner party, as would normally have been done. So we gathered after dinner, conscious of the great courtesy thus displayed by Ronald, who might well have crept off to bed after such a day. We could hardly feel sorry for him, so much, in a way, did he seem to be his old self. He was clearly full of content that he had succeeded, not merely in the physical task of completing and delivering the lecture, but in pleasing and satisfying that large concourse. For the moment, all that seemed to matter was that he was back in

[7] *Ibid.*, p. 54.

Oxford, amongst his Oxford friends, with a great task faithfully executed. The future was as it might be.

Having spent that night in the Vice-Chancellor's lodgings, he left next morning for London, where he was to spend another night at No. 10 Downing Street, where the Prime Minister had invited him to stay, so that he could see Sir Horace Evans. Ronald had been told of his condition, but he was anxious to know, as clearly as the best medical advice could tell him, what the prospects of his doing any more useful work might be.

After he had left Oxford, the Vice-Chancellor's butler came, "pale with anxiety," to tell his master that Ronald had left behind the hot-water bottle which, in the height of June, admittedly an English June, he now needed. The sequel, trivial as it may seem, calls for mention, because it reflects such great credit on the thoughtfulness of busy men. It so happened that the chairman of the University Grants Committee, Sir Keith Murray, had some business with the Vice-Chancellor that day. As he left, to return to London, the Vice-Chancellor told him, "Keith, you've got to take this hot-water bottle to 10 Downing Street."

Although Sir Horace Evans confirmed the diagnosis of cancer of the liver, an inoperable condition, but thought that death would come in a matter of months rather than weeks, Ronald returned to Mells, to all outward seeming, as imperturbable as he had ever been. He had clearly enjoyed the sense of being, however briefly, at the nerve-centre of government, and had been touched by the kindness of Mr. Macmillan and Lady Dorothy. The next morning, the Prime Minister himself took his guest to Paddington ("the station-master was so overcome that he took off his hat twice," reported Ronald) and there took leave of him. Their last conversation must go on record.

"Well, Ronnie, I hope you have a comfortable journey."

"It's a long journey I'm going on."

"I think you're well equipped."

"I hope so."

It was their farewell.

When Ronald was at Eton he had once thought to himself that if he were to take Orders, he would prefer the sort of position which was not likely to demand his attendance at the bedside of the dying. In the two months that elapsed before the end came, it was almost as though he was attending his own deathbed. Since his operation in January, he had been able to say Mass only intermittently and not at all since just before the Romanes Lecture. In a letter in February he had spoken of "all the selfishness, querulousness and general unsupernaturalness which hospital life breeds." Outwardly he seemed increasingly lethargic, despondent and indignant that his body should be thus failing him. Such external manifestations of apparent querulousness as escaped him must be judged in the light of his more considered actions.

One example of his generosity may be given. Throughout his years at Mells, he would complain of the noise made by the church bells in the neighbouring tower. One was never quite sure how much of this had become a kind of humorous pose. Towards the end of his life, the mechanism operating them had ceased to function, and it was necessary to raise funds for their repair. The Rector's plight met with a sympathetic response from Mrs. Asquith and she lent her gardens for a fund-raising effort. Far from dissociating himself from the whole thing, Ronald, ill as he was, took a personal interest in the affair and actually put in a short appearance.

Anxious as always to save other people trouble, he was at pains to arrange all his affairs. His business affairs were set in order, instructions given to his lawyer, his literary executor, his publisher. His wish was to be buried quietly in the church-yard at Mells, but he recognized that a London ceremony would be expected, and he expressed the desire that Father D'Arcy should preach the panegyric which he knew to be inevitable.

From the beginning of July until the 24th of August, the slow process of dissolution dragged on. Unable to eat, unable after August 11th even to receive Holy Communion, he became more and more incapable of the slightest effort. He who all his life had hated the thought of being a nuisance now found himself utterly dependent on the ministrations of others. Even this last purification was to be experienced, this last humiliation to be endured, so that any last traces of self-satisfaction might be eliminated.

Four days after his death, a large company gathered in Westminster Cathedral for the pontifical requiem sung by Bishop Craven in the presence of the Archbishop of West-minster. Few of those present are likely to forget the sermon preached by Father D'Arcy. He who had so often, in such felicitous language, expressed the feelings of mourners and brought out the lesson of the lives of those who had gone, now found one to match his words to the greatness of his theme.

Yet the simple funeral which took place at Mells on August 30th seemed more appropriate than the pomp and splendour of Westminster. He had dazzled and delighted large audiences in his time, and had enjoyed the exercise of his rich and varied talents. But he had been most completely himself, most genuinely happy, in the company of a small group of friends. In the room which was once his chapel in the Old Palace hangs his portrait by Simon Elwes; in his old college of Trinity stands the terracotta head by Arthur Pollen. Neither Eton nor Oxford, neither Shrewsbury nor St. Edmund's, nor a hundred churches and chapels in which he preached, will soon forget him. But his spirit most vividly haunts the grey stone and level lawns and winding lanes of Mells. It was there that he was most completely himself. It was there that his soul was finally made. It is fitting that his mortal remains should there have found their last resting-place.

3

SPIRITUAL GUIDE

WHEN WE TURN to consider the precise and individual qualities of the doctrine of one who has undoubtedly been an outstanding spiritual influence in our generation, we do not find it easy to give the answer. For all the originality and vigour of his mind, he was almost surprisingly orthodox and conventional in his ascetic teaching. He was versed, as we know, in the byways of Christian experience, but his own thinking, his own teaching, was almost wholly formed on the traditional, classical writers. Yet he had a remarkable gift for presenting age-old truths as if they were freshly minted by him. It was not merely that he spoke to his generation in its own idiom. He spoke of something that he had made his own.

It is sometimes said of him, and indeed he used to say himself, that he knew no theology. As we have seen, he was largely self-taught in this field. But granted a mind so perceptive and a disposition so humble and receptive, it is not surprising that his freedom from the pedantries of so much theological teaching enabled him to pierce quickly to the heart of the matter and to keep the minds of his hearers concentrated on essentials. He could relate to these essentials the day-to-day problems of Christian living, but his teaching was always theologically based.

The clearest exposition of his theological approach is to be found, of course, in his *Belief of Catholics*, written in the course of his first year at the Old Palace. But this is a work of apologetic, a defence of the Catholic position against misrepresentation and misunderstanding. If we want to know what theology meant in practice, we must turn to his exposition of it in sermons, in retreats, best of all in his two volumes of conferences delivered to the undergraduates at Oxford—*In Soft Garments* and *The Hidden Stream*.[1] The structure of both works was not accidental. He had himself devised the original plan on which the course was based, and, at a later stage, after he had left Oxford, he was responsible, in collaboration, for the revised version. We can see, therefore, how his mind worked in this field.

There is still a marked strain of the apologetic in his instructions to undergraduates; this was inevitable, in view of the fact that he was helping to prepare them to meet the objections they were likely to encounter from their unbelieving friends. But, all the time, he is building up a picture of what religion is, or should be, to the believer; this is its best and most effective recommendation. All the time he is encouraging his listeners to see life in terms of God, God incarnate. It is the only valid explanation of man's experience.

A few of his aphorisms may help to bring home this development.

[1] New York: Sheed and Ward, 1953.

Whether you want him or not, God is there. You apprehend, with one grasp of the mind, earth's inadequacy and God's all-sufficiency; you see yourself, earthborn, in the true perspective, and read, written in between the lines of all our human record, the attestation of a God whom to acknowledge is to adore.

If you would gauge the difference which revelation has made to our notions of worship, you have only to concentrate on a single *obiter dictum* of Aristotle's. "We should think it very odd," he says, "to hear anybody talking about loving Zeus" . . . It was not till the full revelation came to us that we were spoilt with this sense of a Divine intimacy. I use the word "spoilt" advisedly; for indeed, this sense of intimacy is now something we take for granted.

I have only spoken of the preparation in men's minds. In men's minds, could any more elaborate nest have been built in readiness for the coming of the Dove at Pentecost?

[Of the New Testament] All I have been trying to point out is that it *rings* true. The documents of the New Testament are documents that belong to real life, not an elaborate literary fraud.

Tell me, was he any ordinary Man, the Founder of Christianity, that the recent memory of his unassuming passage through the world should produce such repercussions as these?

Our Lord's claim is not just to satisfy this or that need of common life, meet this or that situation in common life. He offers to give us a new, supernatural life, complete with all its faculties, in the midst of this troubled and precarious world.

. . . If you and I are to be true samples by which the quality of our Church can be judged, we have to be lovers of unity, generous in our dealings with God, generous in our attitude towards men who do not agree with us, and, in some measure as circumstances and opportunities allow, apostoloid.

Your political prejudices, the values you attach to life, don't seem to be as clear-cut, as absolute as they were; is it possible you are becoming broad-minded? But one thing goes on, unaccountably, almost irrationally undisturbed; your faith in the Church as the Body of Christ, and in Christ as the revelation of God. . . . The faith, somehow, has got under your skin; it is there.

. . . the proper, the characteristic food of faith is mystery; when you swim in the full tide of mystery, then your keel is really afloat.

Almighty God has paid us the compliment, which he never paid to the holy angels, of making us a kind of liaison officers between matter and spirit; we've got to accept the things of sense, and to hallow them. To make that difficult job easier for us, he himself took flesh at the Incarnation; and then, by way of continuing the mystery of his Incarnation for all time, gave us the sacraments to link the life of the flesh with the life of the spirit.

The priest himself is a kind of sacrament, a sacrament of fatherhood . . . The priest at the font is the father bringing children to life, supernatural life. The priest at the altar is the father as bread-winner, giving the supernatural family, as it gathers round a common table, its supernatural food. . . . A priest isn't to be thought of as a mere sacrificial beast of burden; as an umbrella-stand to hang your Mass intentions on, or an automatic machine where you put your rosary in and it comes out blessed . . .

There must be a certain abridgement of one's own personality if community life, or married life, is to be a success. But the abridgement of your personality will, commonly at least, be the enrichment of your character.[2]

These passages have been quoted, not merely as affording a kind of skeletonic outline of various aspects of Christian thought, but equally as giving an indication of the quality of Ronald Knox's own approach to the ultimate truths. Sketchy and spasmodic as they are, they can hardly be read without

[2] *The Hidden Stream*, pp. 22, 33, 64-5, 75, 97, 108, 130, 140-1, 174, 184, 201, 213, 216, 227.

giving a sense of absolute conviction, absolute sincerity about the importance, the sacredness of religion in its many aspects. Once again, we come to see how all the early experiences of their author have blended and fused, under the control of God's providence and the working of his grace, to produce a man who saw everything now, not simply *sub specie aeternitatis*, but wholly *in Christo*.

For him the doctrine of the Incarnation was no mere piece of theological antiquarianism; it was seen and shown as fertilizing the life of the Church and her members through that sacramental system of which he was such an effective exponent. Only a life so Christ-centred could have taught as he taught; because he taught things that were, for him, the abiding realities. How many a priest, reading *The Window in the Wall*, has been filled with a kind of holy envy at the mastery of his exposition of eucharistic doctrine and at the fertility of mind which, year after year, in the same church and to much the same congregation, could find something not merely new but absolutely penetrating and enriching to say on this subject! Most priests have two or three sermons on the Blessed Sacrament; here we have close on two score of them, redolent of the preacher's own devotion, and challenging us to a fuller realization of the wealth at our disposal.

Easy to find out where our Lord dwells; but if we would converse with him, be intimate with him, it must be in the obscurity of faith—the veil of the sacramental species hides him from our sight. He demands something of us after all; we must make a venture of faith in order to find him. So accessible to all, and yet such depths of intimacy for those who will take the trouble to cultivate his friendship.

We all know the famous picture of St. John at Ephesus, giving Holy Communion to our Blessed Lady. When we think of that, let us remember that even such love as theirs only found its perfection when it was cemented, not with the memory of Christ dying on the Cross, but the gift of Christ living in the Holy Eucharist.[3]

Not less remarkable is his collection of wedding-sermons, *Bridegroom and Bride*.[4] Here again, the sacramental, theological incarnational aspect of the occasion is always beautifully blended with the tender humanity of a man who, it seemed, could enter into the very hearts of those listening to him at this, the most solemn and the most personal moment in their lives. He had known the riches of human love in his own experience. His dedication to celibacy never meant for him, as it does to some, that marriage seemed "a sort of untidy second best instead of what it is, a splendid vocation and a high sacrament." But he also knew that, whilst the generality of people get sentimental about weddings, the Church is very realistic about human nature. As he had written in *The Hidden Stream*:

She says, "Oh, you want to get married, do you? That means, you want to imitate the action of Jesus Christ in his Incarnation. Well, God bless you; you will want all the grace I can rout out for you if you are to do that, a whole trousseau of graces." She thinks at once, not of the fun you are going to have, but of the qualities you will need.[5]

[3] New York: Sheed and Ward, 1956, p. 25.
[4] New York: Sheed and Ward, 1957.
[5] P. 224.

Nowhere else does Ronald Knox reveal so fully the secret
of his success as a preacher and spiritual guide. For him the
platitudes of the textbook were living realities, because they
referred to living men and women, genuine human situa-
tions.

So, too, is it with his sense of the priesthood. Because he
was aware of the tremendous wealth at the disposal of Christ's
priests, he was not less conscious, partly out of his own self-
examination, partly out of his personal knowledge of seminar-
ies and presbyteries and his personal friendships with so many
priests of every kind, that we do indeed keep this wealth in
frail vessels. Aware of all this, he used the countless opportunities that came his way in the many retreats to priests he
was invited to give, not to exaggerate a burden but to help
to a response to a challenge, not to depress but to console, not
to criticize but to inspire. He did not gloss over the failures of
too many priests; but by contrasting the reality with the glorious ideal, he encouraged even those in danger of disillusion
to renew their hope.

Hagnotes is a quality so pure as to be terrible; it dazzles you;
no embattled array so awes men's hearts. A convoy passing
through a country town, that endless stream of fortified motion,
how it takes your breath away with the realization of the terrible
thing modern war is! Something like that ought to be the purity
of the priest. Not just the insensitiveness of the bachelor, who
finds women a nuisance, not the furtive horror which tries to
forget that sex exists, but something unapproachable, blinding, on
a different plane from thoughts of evil. . . .

The layman who is in a difficulty ought to say to himself, "I'll
go and talk to the priest about it, he'll be able to tell me; *he
knows God.*" The laity at large have the impression, and rightly,

I think, that we priests know our job. I sometimes wonder whether they have the same confidence that we know our Employer.

There is a kind of universal benevolence which sometimes makes itself felt, even in a very shy man, even in a very reserved man, which does win souls. Everybody calls the priest "dear old" Father So-and-So, if not actually "poor old" Father So-and-So; there are no organizations in the parish and the accounts are in a frightful mess, but somehow people go to church. . . .

I think that when our account comes to be audited at the Judgement, the record of the prayers we said will be a surprise for most of us, and, for very many of us, the surprise will not be a disappointment.[6]

So he went on, year after year, encouraging his fellow priests, making them realize that if his life was, in many ways, passed in circumstances different from those obtaining in the average presbytery, this did not mean that he had lost touch with the realities of the priesthood, or had lost sight of them in their multifarious activities. Certainly they felt that they could call on him, as they did, to preach sermons on special occasions—a patronal feast, a consecration, a jubilee.

One of his conferences in *The Priestly Life* is on Our Lady. It concludes with these words:

She is something more to us than a theological symbol. . . . Rather, to each of us, she is a personal romance. Because a natural instinct makes us unwilling to discuss such things in public, I will leave it at that. The real secret of her influence on our lives is something undefined, something undefinable.[7]

[6] *The Priestly Life* (New York: Sheed and Ward, 1958), pp. 28-9, 31, 135.
[7] *Ibid.*, pp. 145-6.

He was, as we know, reserved and undemonstrative, applying the epithet "spinal" to anything that savoured of the sentimental, the uninhibited display of emotion. Yet, from the beginning, he never hid or sought to hide his deep devotion to the Mother of God. We recall the footnote in *A Spiritual Aeneid:*

At the time of my ordination I took a private vow, which I have always kept, never to preach without making some reference to our Lady, by way of satisfaction for the neglect of other preachers.[8]

This was in his Anglican days, but, if the occasion for such references passed with his reception into the Church, the practice persisted.

In defending and developing devotion to Our Lady, he was defending the central truth of Christianity.

Protestants have said that we deify her; that is not because we exaggerate the eminence of God's Mother, but because they belittle the eminence of God. . . . They refuse honour to the God-bearing Woman because their Christ is only a God-bearing Man.

He did much more. He made her live in the minds and hearts of his listeners. As always, in his thought and utterances, theology was pointless unless it bore effectively and fruitfully on the life of the believer.

One further quotation, from a broadcast sermon on the assumption of Our Lady, will suffice to round off this attempt to present the essentials of his treatment of Catholic devotion to her.

[8] P. 86.

When the Son of God came to earth, he came to turn our hearts away from earth, Godwards. And as the traveller, shading his eyes while he contemplates some long vista of scenery, searches about for a human figure that will give him the scale of those distant surroundings, so we, with dazzled eyes looking Godwards, identify and welcome one purely human figure, close to his throne. One ship has rounded the headland, one destiny is achieved, one human perfection exists. And as we watch it, we see God clearer, see God greater, through this masterpiece of his dealings with mankind.[9]

Parallel to his teaching about Our Lady was his study of a whole host of saints. One of his most remarkable achievements as a preacher was his ability to paint a portrait of a familiar saint and bring out some unsuspected aspect of his sanctity. The only possible explanation of the success of his sermons dealing with saints as diverse as St. Thomas Aquinas and St. Bernadette, St. Anselm and St. Philip Neri, was that these were no remote figures, adorning a fresco or assuming quaint attitudes in a stained-glass window; they were very much men and women of our world and our nature. Whilst he was able to draw on his vast historical lore in order to present the saints in their setting, it was his personal devotion to them which made his sermons about them live. Typical of his treatment is this passage from a sermon on St. Edward the Confessor.

Man's happiness lies in devoting himself; his success is the offering he can make. And our Confessor was a successful man, yes, even in this world, because in his simple piety, in the unaffected

[9] *The Pastoral Sermons of Ronald A. Knox:* Edited, with an Introduction, by Philip Caraman, S.J., © Evelyn Waugh, 1960 (New York: Sheed and Ward, 1960).

generosity of his nature, he set himself to serve the men about him by easing their burdens, by relieving their necessities, by confirming them in their allegiance to the faith. Great opportunities passed him by, and he never marked them; he might have altered the dynastic history of England, have left us different manners and a different political constitution, if he had been other than he was. Instead, he left all these things to God's Providence; and God's Providence, using the ambitions of human agents as its puppets, moulded our history beyond man's expectation. And what do they mean to us now, those human agents? Mere names in the history book, mere stiff, attitudinizing figures on the Bayeux Tapestry, they have become part of a past hardly less remote to us than legend. . . . The Conqueror, who diverted the stream of history, went to his grave disappointed and lies there a historical memory. The Confessor, whose ambitions could be satisfied by finding a poor man his dinner, saw no corruption in death, and lives the patron of his fellow countrymen.[10]

"If he had been other than he was," Ronald himself might have done this and that in the literary world, possibly even in the Church. Temperamentally, he may well have seen an affinity between himself and the Confessor, as he certainly shared the Confessor's spiritual outlook. It was not for nothing that he found in the Jesuit writer, De Caussade, one of his favourite spiritual tags "the sacrament of the present moment." Always, he did his best to see in the present situation, the present task, the present interruption of that task the working of a Providence, the hand of a God whom he loved and served. He did not always find it easy; he did not always succeed in repressing the sigh, the slight gesture of impatience, the querulous remark. But this is only to say that he was not

[10] *Occasional Sermons*, p. 28.

perfect; it is not to imply that he did not mean every word he said in these sermons, that he did not try to live the lessons he taught. No one who listened to him as he preached could doubt that here was a man who was setting out an ideal not just for his listeners, but for himself. His capacity for affecting others, by probing into the secret places where we try to hide from ourselves, arose from his own self-knowledge, from his own genuine humility. His effectiveness as a preacher came in the end, not from his skill in language but from his knowledge of the human heart. And the heart he knew best was his own.

When, for example, in a retreat to his fellow priests, he gave them a meditation on "murmuring," he had this to say:

Believe me, you only add to your grievance by taking it out for an airing. It is quite true that it may do good to discuss it calmly with your confessor. Or, very occasionally, it may be your duty to bring something to the notice of a person in higher authority. But to chatter and gossip over your grievances never yet did any good, never yet afforded any real relief; you only hypnotize yourself into imagining your resentment to be stronger than it really is. It is a conspiracy against your own peace of mind.[11]

The man who wrote that passage clearly knew that he was himself exposed to the temptation to air his grievances unduly; but equally it was written by a man still capable of laughing at himself for it, but, even more, capable of seeing the spiritual lesson to be learnt, the spiritual remedy to be applied. Any priest of experience and with a decent measure

[11] *The Priestly Life*, p. 68.

of self-knowledge is all too aware that he is often presenting an ideal which he is far from attaining himself. But he knows too that we are judged on our intentions and genuine efforts. The ideal must present a challenge to all that is highest and noblest in us. The danger, as a rule, is not that we become cynical about our preaching, but that we may become discouraged.

Ronald was aware of this, and in a very valuable meditation on accidie he did his best to console his fellow priests.

You are preparing to go to the altar. You feel certain that all will be as it was yesterday and the day before; there will be no conscious response in you to the sacred words of the liturgy, or even to the near approach of our blessed Lord as he comes to you in holy Communion. It will all be a mechanical routine, like filling in forms. Never mind; you are preparing to offer this lifeless performance to God, all the more hopefully because for you it is a thing without salt; you are doing it, not to please yourself, but to please him. Jesus Christ, our high Priest, is going to offer himself in the Holy Mass, using you as his tool—his dull, uncomprehending tool; you will offer yourself, motionless, into his hands. You will be acting like a conscript soldier under orders, not buoyed up by any foretaste of victory, any consciousness of heroism, but simply doing what he is told. That shall be your sacrifice.

You take up the well-thumbed breviary, and arrange the tattered markers in it. You know well what your office is going to mean; a verse or two read with some sense of what the meaning is about, but alas, with no unction; then a long rumination on your own affairs, starting off at a wide tangent; then the bell that rings in your memory and recalls you to a sense of what you are doing; always the same. A parrot, you feel, would do it as well. To be sure, but at least you can take upon yourselves the duties of God's parrot; the beasts, too, praise God.[12]

The man who could thus speak to his fellow priests was a man who knew, from his own experience, something of the difficulties which the priest encounters. No wonder they found in him stimulus and consolation; no wonder they loved him. Any suggestion that he was regarded by his fellow priests as a kind of sport, someone who did not really belong, who did not know what being a priest was like, is completely at variance with all the evidence. They were proud of him; they were glad that he was enabled by his special circumstances to shed lustre on their common priesthood and on their common religion.

But if he could thus speak from the heart to his colleagues and companions in the priesthood, he could speak with no less effect to every class of listener. Indeed, the secret of his success as a spiritual guide is surely that, whilst he was himself wholly dedicated to the living of a full Christian life, he possessed, at the same time, a remarkable gift for communicating his experience to every type of listener. And this he could do because, shy and reserved as he undoubtedly was, so that strangers sometimes thought him aloof through a sort of arrogance, he possessed an unusual breadth of genuine sympathy and understanding.

That he should appeal to the sophisticated adult is, of course, hardly surprising. Yet his appeal was not the appeal of sophistication, but of something at once much simpler and much more profound. If we look, for example, at the short sermons which he published for years in the *Sunday Times*,

[12] *The Priestly Life*, pp. 77-8.

we find polished epigrams; but the epigrams enshrine some perfectly simple truth. Without in any way seeking to water down or apologize for the full teaching of the Church, he was able by his very conviction to make that teaching, if not acceptable to the reader, at least intellectually respectable and entirely compatible with wit and urbanity. Without compromise, with an insight into human nature that was at times devastating in its directness, he polished and sharpened his goads, his *Stimuli*, until they might pierce the toughest hide.

We moderns are contemptuous of outward appearances; it does not follow that we are humble.

Much easier to find a man who has corrected a tendency to pull his drives than a man who has corrected the habit of uncharitable talk.

Any organized church gives you, not gold waiting to be minted, but ore waiting to be smelted; there will always be dross.[13]

A wholly different audience, yet, as we know, one that loved and cherished his teaching, was the group of schoolgirls who found shelter with him at Aldenham Park. He took the same trouble over preparing his sermons for this unsophisticated congregation as he took over everything he did. They, too, were human beings, entrusted to his spiritual care by a Providence which might well seem, to him and to his friends, to have been playing a mild joke on him. Here he was, all set to translate the Bible in peace and seclusion; into his chosen retreat, almost into the sanctum where he worked, burst this

[13] New York: Sheed and Ward, 1951.

pack of children. If he had been the withdrawn scholar, the superior person of some people's imagination, he would have taken good care to have nothing to do with them. But he was a priest, dedicated first and foremost to the care of the spiritual welfare of human beings, whoever they might be. So, far from hiding behind the smoke-screen of his pipe, he gave them, and us, the *Slow Motion* books.

As we have seen, when he was translating the Little Flower, he talked about getting inside the skin of a "young French female saint." How well he got inside the skin of these young English female scamps! Almost too well, some have felt, put off by the slang and the naïveté of expression. But we know how great was their success with the original audience, and how illuminating many an older person has found them. Even the most sophisticated reader will find something to learn from the following passage, in which the preacher is expounding the difference between what Newman called "notional" and "real" assent.

To *believe* a thing, in any sense worthy of the name, means something much more than merely not denying it. It means focusing your mind on it, letting it haunt your imagination, caring, and caring desperately, whether it is true or not. Put it in this way. If somebody says to you, "Of course, your own country's rule in the Colonies is every bit as brutal as German rule in Poland," you don't reply, "Oh, really? I dare say it is." You care furiously about a statement like that. You may not have the facts at your fingers' ends, but you are not going to let a statement like that pass without examination. It would alter your whole idea of what the world is like if you thought a statement like that could be true. And it has, or it ought to have, the same sort of effect, if somebody tells you that some article of the Christian creed isn't true. . . . If you really *believe* a thing, it becomes part of the make-up of your mind; it lends coherence to your thought, colour to your imagination, leverage to your will. It *matters* enormously. . . .[14]

To him, also, the truth of the Faith mattered enormously. When he spoke to members of the Church—whether they were schoolgirls, undergraduates, pious laity in retreat, members of an ordinary Sunday congregation, groups of specialists attending some official occasion, or priests of God, he spoke to them always in a way that might help them to appreciate more fully their Catholic heritage. Versed as he was in the history of Enthusiasm, appreciative as he was of the contribution to Christian holiness made by men like Wesley or Bunyan, closely as he had studied the French ascetical and mystical writers, he yet knew that his essential task as a priest, apart from administering the sacraments, was to help the ordinary Catholic to understand as far as may be the basic truths of the Church's teaching.

That is why he was prepared to bend his mind to the business of instructing those schoolgirls at Aldenham, translating the language of theology into words of one syllable which they could follow. So he can explain the effects of the Fall.

. . . sometimes we get indigestion, and you will find that with older people, sometimes even with schoolmasters and schoolmistresses, indigestion puts them in a bad temper. Indigestion puts them in a bad temper—do you see what has happened? Indigestion, which is a matter concerned with the body, has given rise to bad temper, which is a matter concerned with the soul. The

[14] *The Creed in Slow Motion* (New York: Sheed and Ward, 1949), pp. 5, 6.

body, which ought to be taking its orders from the soul, is giving its order to the soul instead! That is the kind of thing the Fall has let us in for.[15]

Or this, on the Communion of the Saints:

The floor of heaven is like a window with a muslin curtain across it; we can't see in, but the saints can see out. They see what we are doing and are interested in what we are doing.[16]

So, in a brilliant parable about prayer for the souls in purgatory.

You remember the fable about the lion which was caught in a net, and the mouse that helped it by eating through the net, so that it could get out? You and I are like that when we pray for the souls of Christians departed . . . we can help them, and it isn't presumptuous to think of ourselves as helping them, even splendid people who have fallen gloriously in battle—we are the mice nibbling away at the bonds which hold them, that is all.[17]

"Splendid people who have fallen gloriously in battle." The girls at Aldenham would be thinking about Dunkirk, the Battle of Britain, the other battles of the only war they knew. Can we doubt that he himself was thinking more of the friends who had fallen in France and Flanders nearly thirty years before? As always, his own personal experience came in to reinforce the appeal of traditional teaching.

[15] *Ibid.,* p. 68.
[16] *Ibid.,* p. 199.
[17] *Ibid.,* pp. 200-1.

One of the most important ways in which he brought his personal experience to bear on the question of helping others to develop a genuine spiritual life is to be seen in his various discussions about prayer. Talking about the Holy Ghost, for instance, he has this to say.

I think we sometimes make a mistake about that when our prayers aren't going too well. We try to make a tremendous effort at concentration, try to pump up more energy from somewhere inside ourselves, and reduce ourselves to a better state of prayer by sheer will-power. Whereas I think really the right attitude for us is to fall back more on the Holy Spirit, and leave things more to him. To say, "Go on praying in me, Holy Spirit. I can't do anything, I know I can't do anything, by these frantic efforts of my own. Every time I really try to settle down to it I find myself thinking about the holidays, or about that girl I've quarrelled with, and nothing seems to come. But I *know* it's all right really, because it is *you* who do the praying; I am only a dumb instrument for you to make noises with. Since I find my own efforts make so little difference, let me keep still and leave room for you to go on praying, praying in me."[18]

He needed such encouragement himself, and there can be little doubt that this sort of treatment is far more likely to persuade people to try to pray or not to give up trying to pray than will many of the more formal treatises on the subject. Ronald Knox was not the man to water down the teaching of the Church; but he is insistent that, in this matter, we shall enjoy the freedom of the children of God. So, in his *Retreat for Lay People,* he has this to say:

[18] *Ibid.,* p. 157.

. . . when we are approaching him in the intimacy of our own private prayer, I think he likes it as well as anything else, because it shows more confidence in his understandingness, if we remain silent before him, and let our silence do him honour. No need, even, that any special train of ideas should be passing through our minds, that we should be setting out, even in our silent thoughts, any formula of petition. To keep quiet in his presence, letting our hearts go out to him in utter confidence, in appealing love, in a tender sense of our own unworthiness—that, no less than any formula of words, and perhaps more than any formula of words, is what is really meant by prayer . . . He wants us to use the liberty of the spirit, and come to him boldly, as his children, choosing the prayer that suits us best.[19]

Or, as he puts it in *The Priestly Life,*

Go through the motions of praying, if that is all that you can do, and when you have finished, offer it up to God in a spirit of humility. Tell him he knows your fashioning, knows you are but dust; deplore the natural weakness which makes it so hard for you, his creature, to do the thing you were put into the world to do. Confess to him, at the same time, the habitual want of seriousness and purpose in your life which prevents you attaining recollection when you want it. Tell him you wish your prayer had been one long peaceful aspiration to him; unite it with the prayer of our Blessed Lord while he was on earth, and ask to have it accepted with that mantle cast over it.[20]

Not that, as spiritual counsellor, Ronald Knox was lax or easygoing. Occasionally indeed one senses an excess of strictness in his attitude, as when he says:

[19] Pp. 227, 229.
[20] P. 134.

There's this trouble about doing what God wants us to do—that it's so often, at the same time, the thing that *we* want to do. Even if it's the kind of thing that doesn't sound very attractive at the first go-off . . . it's extraordinary how people get to like it, and take a pride in doing it well, and want to go on doing it. That means we are never quite sure whether we are doing what is God's will because it is God's will or because it is ours.

The answer is, of course, that it is because our natural inclination not infrequently coincides with what is God's will for us that service of God remains basically a reasonable human activity. In private conversation he did at times reveal an attitude of mind bordering on the puritanical; he always seemed to be afraid of letting himself off too lightly.

But, as a general rule, his teaching was in the great classical tradition of the great spiritual writers—the Fathers, St. Thomas, St. Francis de Sales, De Caussade, Newman, to name but a few. And what he learnt from them he tested by his own experience, so that when he came to present it to others it was presented not as something second-hand, but something which appealed to his contemporaries because he had brought it up to date by his own practice of it no less than by his insight into human nature, its needs and its problems.

Thus:

Our Lord said to St. Thomas, "Blessed are those who have not seen, and yet have believed." I dare to hope that he will say to some of us, meeting us in heaven, "Blessed are those who have not felt, and yet have loved."

. . . there are a lot of Christians who do love God, but because

they think they can't love God, never get on to the next thing—
which is giving up their lives and their wills to him.

You see, we men are very curious people. Each of us, in his
heart of hearts, thinks he is right. We seldom take other people's
advice, unless it chimes in pretty accurately with the decision we
had already formed on our own account. Yet we care desperately
what other people think; we cannot be satisfied with the self-
approval of our own conscience, we must for ever be justifying
ourselves in the eyes of our fellow men.[21]

If this chapter seems to be unduly filled with quotation, this
is simply because quotation, and lengthy quotation, seems to
be the only adequate way in which to bring out the quality of
Ronald Knox's spiritual message. Paraphrased, it might seem
almost pedestrian, precisely because it would have lost that
special flavour which his personal idiom alone can confer on
it. Like the "scholar whose learning is of the kingdom of
heaven" he knew "how to bring both new and old things out
of his treasure-house." He, who hated novelties, could invest
age-old truths with a new-minted freshness.

No truth is more hackneyed than the fact of death, one of
the familiar themes of the preacher and retreat-giver. How
often does the priest try to find a fresh approach to this well-
worn theme; how often does he fail. As an example of the
mastery of Ronald Knox, no better illustration can be chosen
than the meditation on death which is given in the post-
humously published *Retreat for Beginners*.

It begins, quite cheerfully, with a story about an old gentle-
man who enjoys his meals and has plenty of money and is
inclined to think the world isn't such a bad sort of place.

[21] *Retreat for Lay People*, pp. 81, 78, 102.

Being granted three wishes, he chooses, for his first wish, the gift of immortality. But this turns out to be not quite what he wanted, so he goes on to ask to be allowed to die, but at a moment of his own choosing; "nothing was to happen to him until he said the word, Go." At first this is all satisfactory enough, until he begins to realize that, whilst he really wants to be dead, he is afraid of dying.

For those who are unfamiliar with the meditation, it will spoil their fun to go on with the story. But we can have no kind of doubt that by now the schoolboys listening to him were all agog, and that he could go on to develop the theme, certain that his listeners would go on listening. It is the final paragraph which brings out the attitude of mind with which he hoped that they would accept their death, an attitude of mind which manifestly expresses his own spirit.

And now all that is over, because death has come; and we wrap it all up in a parcel, as it were, and thrust it towards him, like a bad piece of knitting, for his acceptance. "Take it, Lord; I know I've made a mess of it again and again, this life you gave me to live; the pattern hasn't been your pattern, and there have been loose edges everywhere. But it was *meant* to be like your Son's life, a sacrifice; take it, please, and make what you can of it; I have come to the end of the skein now."[22]

[22] © Evelyn Waugh, 1960 (New York: Sheed and Ward, 1960), p. 198.

II

RONALD KNOX THE WRITER

by Robert Speaight

To Elizabeth Wansbrough

I

THE WRITER
AND HIS AUDIENCE

OF HOW MANY ORDAINED MINISTERS of the Catholic Church
in England can you say that they were professional writers,
in the accepted meaning of the term? Of none can it be said
without qualification, since writing could not, in the nature of
their case, be the principal end of their activity. Nevertheless,
we admire Newman as a master of English prose, and we
allow to Robert Hugh Benson his niche among the minor
English novelists. No one, it is true, could describe Gerard
Manley Hopkins as a professional poet—but then is there
such a thing as a professional poet? And Hopkins is revered as
a poet by many people who would not think of revering him
as a priest. These men all wrote for the pleasure, as well as for
the purpose, of writing, and they all invite a literary judgment. It is the contention of this essay that Ronald Knox
stands, not necessarily on the same level as they do, but in the
same company. And among his ecclesiastical contemporaries
he stood virtually alone.

In the winter months of 1961 I found myself on a lecture

tour in the United States. Since I was under academic and not
under commercial auspices, I had a good deal of time on my
hands, and I employed this to read—or in many cases to re-
read—the works of Ronald Knox. I particularly remember a
week-end in Erie, Pennsylvania. There is not much to be said
about Erie, except what is said about it by the local population—that it is "a mistake by the lake." But among the rare
amenities of the place is Mercyhurst College for Women
(young girls), whose hospitality I was privileged to enjoy.
Between Saturday and Monday I read *God and the Atom*, the
most prophetic reaction to Hiroshima to have been uttered in
the English language; the account of the Quakers and the
Anabaptists in *Enthusiasm*, a long book of more than six hundred pages which Knox regarded as his *magnum opus*—a
work of *haute vulgarisation* unique in the scope of its enquiry; *The Belief of Catholics*, a standard manual of apologetics; and *The Viaduct Murder*, a detective story which is in
the same class as *Trent's Last Case*, if some way below it. And
in my luggage I had two fat volumes of *Sermons*. That is
what I mean by a professional writer—and, incidentally, by a
professional reader as well.

When, a few lines from the opening of *The Viaduct Murder*, you come across the following sentence:

Pastor Oatvile (distrust the writer whose second paragraph does
not come to ground in the particular) . . .

you know that you have to do with an old hand, and one
whose pen will not disdain an occasional flourish. In fact, you
may safely assume that if Ronald Knox had not been a priest,
he would still have been a writer; and you may doubt

whether, if he had been unable to go on writing, he would
ever have been a priest. For writing was the chief tool of his
apostolate. Those who listened to his sermons, conferences
and retreats may object that here the instrument was rather
the haunting presence and the living voice—a trifle languid, a
shade monotonous, but curiously compelling; yet they will
soon remember the typescript loose on his knees if he were
sitting down, or discreetly visible on the lectern or pulpit if he
were standing up. The last time I heard him speak in public
was at a luncheon at the Hyde Park Hotel to celebrate his
translation of the Bible. He was naturally the guest of honour
and in due course he responded to the toast proposed by
Cardinal Griffin. It was without exception the wittiest after-
dinner speech I have ever listened to, and every word of it
was written down. He told me afterwards that it had taken
him two weeks to prepare.

Books were in his blood, and he tells us that he was already
writing hymns in the nursery. He never made any bones
about preferring Protestant hymns to Catholic ones; perhaps
that was why he neglected this form of composition after his
conversion. But three-quarters, or more, of what he wrote
was designed, not indeed to be sung, but to be spoken aloud;
and before it appeared in print it had stood the test of performance. Now it is a commonplace of criticism to say of a
writer that he has an ear for rhythm. Belloc said it, and with
reason, of himself. But the ear must be unusually sharp when
it has to approve, so to speak, the sound of its own voice. A
dramatist writes for actors, and the actors will pretty soon
let him know if his lines are difficult to speak. It is not, of
course, in the least a question of naturalistic dialogue. Neither
the dialogue of Shakespeare nor the dialogue of Shaw is

naturalistic; but both are easy to speak. Nothing is less naturalistic than the oratory of Burke; yet his Corinthian eloquence is equally effective on the platform and on the printed page. Moreover, if the greater part of what a writer commits to paper is meant for oral delivery in his own person, then his purely literary production will tend to have the same ease of rhythm, the same immediacy of communication. The sense of an audience—of its expectations, its capacity, and its impatience—will be with him all the time.

Now Ronald Knox had in a high degree this awareness of an audience. He will not waste words and he will not waste time. He knows that a live, as distinct from a literary, audience cannot go back upon its tracks and pick up, or disentangle, the threads of what he is saying to them. He must make his meaning clear to them at once, or not at all. A congregation cannot listen to a sermon as a graduate student will read *The Waste Land* or *The Anathemata* with his eye on a B. Litt. The value of reading these, and similar hermetic masterpieces, may well depend on our perseverance in reading them for the twentieth time. But Ronald Knox was far too realistic and far too modest to assume that anyone would want to read him for the tenth, let alone the twentieth time— though in fact some of us may do so. That, however, is not because we are uncertain of his meaning, but because he has said something so perfectly that we long to hear him say it again. For himself, he was content if the undergraduates at Oxford did not cough, and if the boys at Ampleforth did not shuffle, and if the girls at Aldenham did not sneeze—and if you and I did not stifle a suppressed yawn. If he were to hold our attention in the pew, or in the corner of the railway carriage, or in the depths of our favourite armchair, he knew that he must be lucid, and that, as far as his context allowed, he must also do his best to be lively. It is not so easy to be lively when you are discussing the aberrations of the Albigenses or the eccentricities of the Anabaptists; but I have read in fairly quick succession practically everything that Ronald Knox ever wrote, and although some things have interested me more than others, I have not found in all his work a dull or an obscure paragraph. Yes, he was a very professional writer indeed.

Le style—c'est l'homme même; Buffon's aphorism is all very well, but it would be a poor compliment to a man who cared so deeply about the matter of his writing to concentrate uniquely upon the manner of it. Some people—but they are not the best writers—wear their style like a fancy waistcoat. Ronald Knox wore his like a glove. It fitted exactly what he was saying. It never flapped at the fingers or rumpled at the wrist. Yet it was too elegant—even, on occasion, too studied —to be quite unobtrusive. It had been bought in Bond Street. But Ronald Knox (to desert the metaphor) never lets you forget what he is saying in the pleasure you take in his way of saying it. And just as you cannot separate the manner from the matter, so you cannot separate either from the man. I wish to trespass as little as possible on ground which more properly belongs to his biographer. But if the bulk of Ronald Knox's writing is a man talking to an audience—to many varieties of audience—then we shall be in no way to appreciate the pith and precision of his writing unless we understand what those audiences were, and something at least of the man who spoke to them.

The luncheon at the Hyde Park Hotel, to which I have already referred, saw him happily and definitively in his setting. He was by now an ageing man in his middle sixties, not by any means worn out, but past the prime of his activity. His most important work, undertaken at the request of the English Hierarchy, had been accomplished. He was surrounded by friends and admirers, most of whom would have referred to him—even when they did not address him—by his Christian name. He was, in the most literal sense of the word, a familiar figure. Never within miles of being a leader of the English Catholics, he had yet become, in a very special and a very personal way, their representative. The wit of the Oxford Common Rooms and the slightly perplexed incumbent of the Oxford Chaplaincy had mellowed, not into a sage or an elder statesman, but quite simply into a friend. His voice, at once so diffident and so decisive, made you think of Newman, even though you had never listened to Newman. Like Newman, he had migrated from the quadrangle into the cloister, if we may extend the cloister to include the church of which it is a part. He was sensitive like Newman, and we have learnt from his biographer that he was tried by authority in ways unsuspected even by those who knew him best. But he lacked altogether the self-pity which was Newman's besetting temptation. For all his intellectual subtlety, he was spiritually robust.

Yet he was not, as Newman was, an intellectual pioneer; nor did he emulate the mandarin splendours of Newman's style. If new ideas were to be mooted and new syntheses to be constructed, that task was not for him. He did not regard himself as an expert theologian; here he was generally content with traditional rulings. For the rest, he was satisfied to walk in the well-trodden paths of piety, with the *Imitation* as his slightly formidable guide. A humble man, always conscious of the Christian risk, you may say (if you like) that he played for safety. Souls must be saved, his own and other people's, even at a high cost in prudence. You may also say that he was constantly on guard against his own cleverness. The result, where his writing was in question, was no lack of surface brilliance when this was to the point; but there was a corresponding gain in depth. Compare his *Occasional Sermons* with Newman's. You may prefer one or the other, but you cannot say Knox's are the more brilliant. Compare his controversial method with Newman's *Difficulties of Anglicans*. You may rejoice in Newman's exultant irony, but the muting of this in Knox—though there is no blunting the edge of argument—may appeal more quickly to your sympathy; and may well have proved more persuasive to Protestant ears.

He was a man of strong and special loyalties, but he did not attach himself to any one of the spiritual families of which English Catholicism was composed. The Benedictine peace, the Jesuit enterprise, the Dominican audacity—all of these received his tribute, none of them claimed his preference. He might, one thinks, have made a natural and happy Oratorian, and he always remembered with gratitude the hospitality of the London Oratory in the days just after his conversion. One guesses, though he nowhere says so, that the Oratory was his favourite church. But it was from the more humdrum ranks of the secular clergy that he rose to his unique position; "as easily at home"—the words were Cardinal Griffin's—"in the humblest presbytery as at the High Tables of Oxford or Cambridge." To this sympathy for the seminary mill he owed it that he could speak for everyone on every imaginable occasion. Perhaps you were attracted by Newman and repelled by Faber; Ronald Knox saw the point—because he had learnt to

see the point—of both. You expected him to appreciate St.
Thomas More; but were you surprised at his devotion to St.
Philip Neri?

No, he was as Catholic in his sympathies as the Church
herself, and for that reason he was so well qualified to speak
for her. This man of exceptional mind, reared in the heart of
Protestant and patrician England, seemed to devote his whole
capacities to the interpretation of what is rather loosely called
"the mind of the Church." Of his biblical scholarship and
pastoral theology I shall only be qualified to speak in so far
as they released his literary powers; my point here is that he
was, consciously at least, an interpreter rather than an in-
novator. The clergy and hierarchy, though they may have
had some initial doubts, were not afraid of what this brilliant
young man from Balliol might be going to say next. They
admired, they trusted, and they loved him—that was the impression you took away from the luncheon at the Hyde Park
Hotel. His political opinions—as far as he had any—were confined to a rather old-fashioned patriotism and a dislike of government interference. If you have been born into the top
class, I suppose you are particularly sensitive to the fact of
your country no longer being the top country. This seemed
to bother Ronald Knox rather more than it bothered his
younger contemporaries, and he had a way of referring wist-
fully to the relief of Ladysmith. His social habits were also
conservative. But this insularity never prevented him feeling
at one with a European culture which spoke with many
tongues and with the religion that had formed it. His sense of
history was acute and did something to make up for his
morbid disinclination to travel. First and foremost, however,
he was a priest, and that must be understood if we are to

understand the achievement, and also the limitations, of his writing. Ecclesiastically speaking, he was neither to the right nor to the left. He was central; he was representative; and he was unique.

But if, you may argue, Ronald Knox was simply the Public Orator of English Catholicism, does he really merit an excursion into literary criticism? If the reader is spurred to seek an answer to that question in Ronald Knox's writings, this book will have served its purpose. But of course he was much more than that. He spoke, as occasion offered, to a wider public— on the radio, in the Press. He debated regularly at the Oxford Union. He contested, with vigour and skill, the heresies of the hour. He won, eventually, an argument with Sir Arnold Lunn. He might, it is true, have addressed the Anglicans rather differently—have said, either to himself or to the professors at St. Edmund's, "I understand the Anglican and Protestant mentality a good deal better than the common run of Catholics. If one is to convert these people, one has got to get their wave-length. They are much more Catholic than many Catholics suppose. What they object to is our idiom rather than our dogma—our legalism, our plaster statues, our mumbled Masses, our Mediterranean piety, even what appears to them our superstition. If, without any doctrinal compromise, we could make the Church *in* England look a little more like the Church *of* England, might not England be converted more quickly? Might not I, with my Anglican antecedents, act as a kind of bridge, interpreting the Church of England to the Church of Rome as well as the Church of Rome to the Church of England: emphasising the things that unite us rather than the things that divide?"

He might have argued thus, with the best intentions, and

possibly with beneficial results. But he did not in the least want to be a bridge; an Anglican can hear the word too often. He was never interested in preaching an easy Catholicism—a Catholicism without garlic, if you like, seasoned to the palates of All Souls. Protestants must take the Church as he had taken her—as she was. Let others—a von Hügel perhaps—build their bridges with the Church of England. He would not, in historical honesty, say anything which might persuade anyone to be contented with a portion of the truth when he knew that only the whole could satisfy them. The Catholic Church was not a haven for foreigners and special temperaments; it was a place where all humanity should be at home. And so he did not content himself with preaching the essence of the Faith; he preached its accidents as well. He spoke as the member of a family—and he was a man to whom families were precious—giving to his listeners something more than the ground plan and elevation of the house; showing them its furniture and its furbelows, its accumulated junk, its happy disorder—with some intimate snapshots of its inmates.

In fact, his audience was far wider than the English Catholics he represented, or even the mass of educated Englishmen to whom he appealed. How wide, he probably realised only when his American royalties came in. Resolutely, over the years, he had refused to go to America; partly because he was so averse to travelling, partly because he doubted whether America would like him, and perhaps, chiefly and secretly, because he doubted whether he would like America. Let no American take offence at this. Ronald Knox was a shy man; he really only enjoyed the society of his friends and the landscape of the United Kingdom. Yet how often have I not sought for his books on the shelves of an American college library and found most of them in circulation! How many the questions that have been put to me about him! How eager and affectionate the curiosity! Where Belloc is all but forgotten and even Chesterton a little receded from view, Ronald Knox speaks to Catholic America through his nervous and sinewy prose, and the pure spirituality it distils. The American reader does not see, because he cannot imagine, the inexportable product of the Balliol tradition; but he hears a voice, prophetic as the voice of Newman, whose message is universally relevant and universally understood. There are scores of Newman societies in the United States; but do they read Newman? The *Apologia* perhaps, but not much else. They read Knox.

I am writing as though Ronald Knox were exclusively a preacher and an apologist; but of course he was a humanist as well. Generally he wrote to illustrate and defend the Faith of his adoption; but more than occasionally he wrote for fun. He never wrote better than when he was writing for fun, and there was a public for his satires which he would never have expected for his sermons. He probably wrote better classical verse than any other scholar of his day, with the possible exception of Dean Inge: and that secured for him a select academic audience. The prize-winning flash and ease of a First in Greats[1] became accessible to a wider, but still an educated, public when he employed the methods of the Higher Criticism to demolish the authenticity of *The Return of Sherlock Holmes*, or took his readers for a ramble in Barsetshire. No acquaintance with either theology or literature was required to identify *The Footsteps on the Lock*, and it was a more than average popular credulity which turned his broadcast com-

---

[1] *Litterae Humaniores:* the Oxford examination in philosophy.

mentary on the English Revolution into a *succès de scandale*. The humanist and the Christian in Ronald Knox were easy bedfellows, and the urbanity of his writing owed a good deal to this alliance. You do not ever feel with him the tension that you feel with Newman, that you feel overwhelmingly with Hopkins. Ronald Knox might have been described as a sad man; but if he was a strained man, he rarely showed it. The lightness that he could bring to his treatment of the sacred was matched by the seriousness he brought to his treatment of the profane. Like an actor who knows how to make his points without effort and to get his laughs without going on his knees for them, Ronald Knox, when he sat down to his type-writer, knew just what he wanted to do—and did it.

2

THE HUMANIST

I HAVE SAID that Ronald Knox was a Christian and a humanist:
I was careful not to describe him as a Christian humanist. The
distinction is not entirely pedantic. When you describe a man
as a Christian humanist you may be suspected of implying,
perhaps quite wrongly, that his Christianity is modified, be it
never so little, by his humanism; that the absolutes of his faith
are blurred by the relativities of his culture. The description is
better avoided altogether in the case of a man so dedicated to
the supernatural as Ronald Knox. Heaven knows, the twentieth century has need of humanists. Nevertheless, we should
not forget that humanism has often been preached as an alternative, if not as an enemy, to Christianity—Professor Huxley's "scientific humanism" is a case in point—and that when a
man tells you he is a humanist, he may very well be telling
you, politely and evasively, that he is not a Christian. Unable,
or unwilling, to accept the Word of God, he is trying to
make do with the word of man. It is because Ronald Knox
was never tempted, at any stage of his development, by this
ersatz that he was able to keep his humanism healthy and his
faith pure and undefiled.

In a letter to a friend who had lent him a book by Ronald Knox—it was, if I am not mistaken, *Memories of the Future* —Belloc brusquely commented: "Knox is thin and he is insufficiently coarse." The judgment has the ring of parody, and it was certainly not Belloc's last word on the work of one whom he deeply respected as a writer, revered as a priest, and loved as a friend. It was uttered before he had read *Let Dons Delight*. Nevertheless it is worth asking ourselves how much it contained of truth. You may put it the other way round and admit that no one could have called Ronald Knox full-blooded: yet even here appearances were deceptive. You thought of him, perhaps, as a man of low physical vitality, a likely victim to accidie. And then you remembered his skillful wielding of a scythe, his precise manipulation of a punt; you knew that he liked going for walking tours; you recalled the sheer amount of work he always managed to get through. No, Belloc's judgment only holds good if you confuse vitality and noise; if you forget that vitality can just as well express itself in concentration and in quiet.

Knox was a quiet man and he often seemed to be a tired man, but you would never say that his writing lacks vitality. It never goes slack. On the other hand, you could never describe him as other than refined, in the sense that he was extremely civilised; and this reticence was apparent in his work. It was a form of literary good manners. It goes without saying that he was morally sensitive, but he was also morally fastidious—and this would have precluded him from dwelling on certain themes, and from the use of certain language, even if he had not been writing as a priest. Where you and I would say "damned" he, to the end of his days, would say "dashed" —and he was probably the last man in England to say it. Nor was this a period affectation; it was due to his belief that damnation was a desperately serious business. His refinement was not a false and finicky refinement, but it did, I think, cut him off from certain areas of reality. There were some authors he would not read because they were too sensual, and others because they were too sophisticated. He was happier with Jane Austen and Trollope.

All this is only to say that he was faithful to a code of manners and of morals which he had learnt in an excellent but rather conventional Christian home; and that this was reflected in his writing. He was an artist, but he was nothing of an aesthete. He liked to be comfortable—you may even say that he liked to be cosy—but he was not bothered by good taste. His books, his pipe, his Breviary, his typewriter, his pack of cards for Patience—these were his properties, whatever may have been his *décor*. He had no eye for pictures and no ear for music, but his feeling for landscape, particularly of southern England, recalled the *pietas* of Virgil —and that takes us straight to the heart of his humanism. For Ronald Knox was a humanist in the sense that More and Colet and Erasmus were humanists: he was a man whose canons of literary judgment were formed by a close acquaintance with the masters of classical antiquity. And the point to emphasise here is not so much that he came under their influence at an early age and remained under it; but that he knew them so well that they did not take him in.

Most authors regard their *juvenilia* in the light of moral indiscretions, but they must be held to them if we are to judge their development. At the time when Ronald Knox went up to Oxford it was normal for a young writer to give his book a Latin title, even if it had nothing to do with the classics.

Juxta Salices was published by Alden & Co. at Oxford in
June 1910, and is now a rare literary curiosity. It was dedicated, generally, to "all Old Etonians, Good Churchmen,
and Smokers of Briar Pipes"—a category in which the author
himself would always have been proud to be included; and
particularly to his friend Patrick Shaw-Stewart, soon afterwards to be killed in the First World War. In view of Ronald
Knox's staunchly conservative opinions and the kind of
patrician halo which aureoles so many of that gifted and fated
generation, it is worth remembering that Shaw-Stewart, like
Rupert Brooke, called himself a Socialist. In the following
lines Knox evokes his comradeship:

> Oxford has given me friends to choose,
> Others have sympathised at need,
> Agreed more wholly with my views—
> But you, you only still succeed,
> Without admonitory pokes
> In understanding all my jokes.

The miscellany of *Juxta Salices* was culled from *The Corn-
hill*, *The Oxford Magazine*, *The Isis*, *The Eton College
Chronicle*, and *The Outsider*. The first of these periodicals, at
least, suggests a broadening market for Knox's literary ven-
tures. His heart is still at Eton, and we find him celebrating
the retirement of the School Clerk with one of those cheerful
allusions to corporal punishment without which no reminis-
cence of the English Public Schools is ever complete:

> Clerk in Scholastic Orders! Can I deem
> Thy last roll called, thy final victim beaten,
> Thou passest from thy glory, who did'st seem
> The most unaged in all unaging Eton.

It was in the sacristy, not in the stews, that Ronald Knox sowed his wild oats; the Church of England was already becoming the target for his private jokes at a time when it was at least as important what a clergyman should wear as what he should believe. The following may well be the only poem ever to be composed about an ecclesiastical tailor:

> CUCULLUS FACIT MONACHUM
> Quickly the Church's seasons change,
>   "Mutamur nos in illis";
> Hasten, ye vicars, to arrange
>   With Messrs. Jones & Willis.
>
> See where he stands, that fervent soul,
>   The Reverend Michael Dolan,
> Accoutred in a Lenten Stole
>   That is not lent nor stolen!
>
> The band around his shoulders slim
>   Is of the very purplest,
> For Jones & Willis cassocked him
>   And Jones & Willis surpliced.

For sheer prize-winning cleverness it would be difficult to beat Knox's entry in the Visitors Book at Hartland Quay on the rugged north coast of Devon. Corydon speaks and Echo takes up the refrain, answering the question at the same time: here are three examples:

Corydon: What, Echo, shall I find at Hartland Quay,
         Save walls abandoned long ago and sea?
Echo: Go and see.

Corydon: How shall I reach (for wind and wave are fickle)
          Those fields untouched by harrow or by sickle?
Echo: Bicycle.
Corydon: What of mine host? for if the host be rude,
          The fare, whate'er it be, is none so good?
Echo: None's so good.

But the most elaborate contribution to the volume is an imaginary symposium on the subject of love, held in Balliol. This was actually performed one evening by the Decalogue Society, each member being assigned the character least inappropriate to him. Dr. Johnson observes to Bernard Shaw, "Sir, you throw the aegis of a philosophy which none but you could adopt, over a pornography which none but you could appreciate"—to which Mrs. Malaprop rejoins: "He says he throws the haggis of a philosophy over a photography which none but he could depreciate." Dr. Johnson observes, in another context, "Sir, the man who would write his own life is either afraid of the judgment of posterity, or too poor a creature to find a biographer": and Sam Weller, tiring of the discussion, remarks, "Quite enough for vun evening, as the old gent said when he gave it up and slept on the landing." When Socrates pins Sam down with the question: "Come, come, this is a triangle, is it not?", Sam replies: "I'm villing to take anything from you, sir; as the highwayman said to the guard, ven he held up the stage coach." Mrs. Malaprop finds herself at odds with Sir Roger de Coverley over the intimacies of the young. "Nevertheless, I hold that such intricacy does not become a young woman. I would not have her acquainted with any male society till she should have reached years of depression . . . I would have her kept by her parents as straitly as Daniel in the Brazen Tower; and when the time came, they should find her an illegible husband to lead her to the halter." And when Socrates asks whether the time has not come "when we ought no longer to discuss the aspects of love and its limits, but rather see if we cannot discover itself in itself what it is, and for this purpose relinquish no clue, till like good sleuth hounds we have run the runaway Eros to earth?"—Sherlock Holmes tersely intervenes—"You will find all the clues in the left-hand top drawer of the large pigeon-hole desk. They are marked Moriarty." Here is the supreme parodist of *Absolute* and *Abitofhel* moving quickly into his stride.

No complex of inferiority is more acute than that of a man destined for Winchester, who was not clever enough to go there with a scholarship and was doubtfully clever enough to go there without one. So I probably have an exaggerated respect for a classical education. I instinctively want to genuflect when I meet a man who can read Demosthenes without a dictionary. I realise, of course, that a great deal of classical education is mere pedantry and that it breeds a particularly sterile form of academic snobbery. A man may turn an elegant hexameter and yet have no literary discrimination whatever. He may remember every phase of the Peloponnesian War and yet be devoid of any historical sense. He may know his Aristotle and yet have no judgment in applying him. It is easier for a camel to pass through the eye of a needle than for a scholar of Balliol to admit that there is anything more important than a First in Mods.[1] But Ronald Knox, even when he went up to Balliol, realised that man was not made for Mods.

[1] Honour Moderations, an examination taken by those studying Greek and Latin towards the end of their second year at Oxford.

Nevertheless, in the days of his most spectacular pot-hunting —as an envious contemporary might have put it—a classical education still maintained its traditional prestige. If you described a man as a brilliant scholar, you implied that he was a classical scholar. At a time when his promotion to a bishopric might depend on his class in Schools, there was nothing even superficially incompatible between the classics and Christianity. It is hardly an exaggeration to say that his syntax was as important as his sanctity, and that the "unseen" mattered more than the Unseen.

A classical education, then, may deflect its subject in two directions; in the direction of pedantry or in the direction of paganism. Ronald Knox was a punctilious scholar, but he was no pedant; and he was nothing, either, of a romantic Hellenist. He saw that the romantic Hellenist, like other romantics, only sustained his romanticism by leaving a great many things out of account. In exalting this, he excluded that. Here indeed he has something in common with the romantic medievalist. For the one, the whole story is in the beautiful statue; for the other it is all in the stained-glass window. Ronald Knox was not particularly sensitive to either, but he was intensely interested in how men and women thought and acted at a given time and why. Men and women mattered more than the most marvellous of their works, because they had immortal souls. And so it is not surprising that if we want to get at the heart of Ronald Knox's humanism, we have to turn not only to his occasional essays but to his *Occasional Sermons;* and turn, also, to some of his earliest lectures, which were delivered in 1912 when he was Chaplain and Fellow of Trinity College, Oxford; and was only twenty-four years old.

These have never been published—an omission which I find more inexplicable with every passing year. Their subject is Virgil, and it was in my capacity as President of the Virgil Society that I had the opportunity of reading them. They had been lent to the monastic library at Ampleforth by one who had himself heard them and to whom they now belong. Since Ronald Knox had been a faithful member of the Virgil Society since its inception during the Second World War, I had been asked to deliver a lecture in his memory, and these lectures—kindly lent to me by their owner—gave me all the material I needed. They had been delivered to undergraduates, not without an eye to the General Paper in Honour Moderations. It was easy to see how they would have "got across" to the same kind of audience that followed Ronald Knox's Conferences at the Oxford Chaplaincy—followed them regularly three times a year long after he had ceased to be its Chaplain. There is the same wit and incisiveness, the same common sense of a very uncommon mind, the same felicity in finding a contemporary illustration, the same ease of expression. Here is the Knox who squatted with so assured an air of possession in Baker Street or Barchester; the satirist who was without a peer in his generation, because he knew so much about certain people's minds. For satire, like parody which is one of its forms, depends upon sympathy as well as upon criticism. And we are fortunate in the fact that Ronald Knox probably had a warmer sympathy for Virgil than he had for any other poet. Where that sympathy led him the lectures illustrate very clearly.

Knox was certainly a Virgilian scholar—and a fine one. He could hold his own, sometimes rather caustically, with the commentators, offering his own theories and emendations. He

is not frightened by Conington, whom he found rather elaborate, or by Sedgwick, whom he found excessively pompous;
and when Coleridge tells us that when you take away the
metre and the melody of Virgil you "have nothing left," he
tells Coleridge where he gets off. Behind the subtlety and
shyness of Ronald Knox there was an almost alarming self-
confidence. In this, as in certain other respects, he was not
unlike Cardinal Newman, and it is good to know that the
busts of these two great Christian humanists—one cannot,
after all, avoid the word—are now keeping each other company in Trinity. But Knox was something more important
than a Virgilian scholar; he was, again like Newman, an *anima
naturaliter Virgiliana*. We all have a certain idea of what we
mean by Virgilian. As I look out of my study window on to
the rolling orchards and hop-fields of the Kentish weald, I
often say that the landscape is Virgilian. I say the same thing
—and Knox said it too—when I look at the background of an
Italian Pre-Raphaelite, and see the towers of some Tuscan
hill-town silhouetted against the sky. There is—we all know
it—a sadness and a gentleness in Virgil, a quiet melancholy
and dissatisfaction, a nostalgia for he knows not what, a
tremulous alertness, as if there had just reached him, borne
faintly on the breeze, the music of the spheres. Ronald Knox
was the most unmusical of men, and perhaps this last analogy
would have made small appeal to him. Newman, however,
would have understood it; and though I am not one of those
who would baptize Virgil by a process of total immersion, I
think that he prefigured in his temperament and his predispositions a type of Christian humanist of which Knox and
Newman were examples. He may have believed the Roman
urbs to be much more abiding than in fact it proved to be—

though it stood a good while by modern standards; but it was surely not for nothing that Aeneas descended into the underworld, and that it was upon a vision of things seen only by the eye of imagination and piety that Virgil launched his prophecy of the Augustan peace.

Ronald Knox had a great deal to say about that wonderful supernatural guess which almost lifts the Sixth Book of the *Aeneid* into the realm of natural theology, but he began, quite literally, with the alphabet, telling us that we must spell Virgil with two *'i'*s. I seem to remember that at my private school we spelt Virgil with an 'e,' but Knox went on to adjure his listeners to forget everything they had been told about Virgil at their private schools. He reminded them that a great poem only begins to live with the death of its author, and that to understand Virgil you must appreciate not only the influence which earlier literature had upon him, important as that influence may have been—particularly Homer—but the influence that he had upon the literature that came after him. He was like old port; a comparison that even the Junior Common Room at Trinity might have been expected to appreciate. "As you drink it not gulping but rolling it round the tongue, you are reminded, not of the sunny fields from which the original fruit was gathered, the impression left by champagne" (I repeat, this was in 1912, when undergraduate familiarity with champagne was greater than it is today) "but the long vigil in the cool cellars which it has kept since it was first laid down." There was St. Augustine who said that the thought of Dido "exstinctam, ferroque extrema secutam" affected him like the peril of his own soul; and Savonarola who declared that the mere magic of a single line heu fuge crudeles terras, fuge litus avarum

confirmed his resolution to retire into the cloister. There was
Voltaire who remarked that if there were any truth in the
saying that "Homer made Virgil," then Virgil was the best
thing that he had made; and there was Burke who had him as
his bedside book; and Michelet who called him holy; and
Bossuet who knew him by heart. It was not until the nineteenth century that the fame of the *Aeneid* was clouded by
critical conceit. "Bede," said Knox "understood Virgil, because Bede took the Christian religion on trust from other
people; Hegel did not understand Virgil, because Hegel
found it necessary to invent the Christian religion all over
again for himself. Burke understood Virgil because Burke was
content to write English; Carlyle did not understand Virgil
because Carlyle insisted on writing Carlylese." It was of the
essence of some of Virgil's most famous lines that they had
not the least idea, so to speak, how famous they were to become; it is we, not Virgil, who load them with tremendous
meanings. *Facilis descensus Averno* was a perfectly straight-
forward way of saying that it was easier to get into Tartarus
than to get out of it. Yet a leader in *The Daily Mail* had
quoted this as a warning against national degeneration; and
The Spectator had used *non tali auxilio* as a weapon against
Tariff Reform; and an elderly clergyman had written to *The
Church Times* applying *timeo Danaos* to the education policy
of a Liberal Government.

By this time an audience even of reluctant Latinists was
well awake and prepared to follow Knox's analysis of the
politics and the passions of Book Four. Aeneas was not made
to desert Dido simply because Virgil had got his hero—and

himself—into a hole, and this was the only way to get them out of it. Nor was the desertion merely an excuse for declamation. Aeneas had deserted Dido because Aeneas was Julius Caesar and Dido was Cleopatra. This was the kind of thing that Augustus, and the contemporaries of Augustus, would have remembered; when monarchs abdicate, or look like abdicating, the public doesn't easily forget it. "And what better compliment," asked Knox, "could Virgil pay to Augustus than to remind him that he was the heir of a man who in such circumstances had responded to the call of duty, and the conqueror of one who, in the same circumstances, had ignobly left the call unanswered?" Knox was concerned to stress the meaning of the Augustan peace, and the nature of the *Aeneid* as a peaceful epic—for all its loud and incidental combat—written at a time when a peaceful epic was almost a contradiction in terms. The poets of the Augustan age had seen the world turned upside down, and they could appreciate the benefits of order. Virgil was pre-eminently the poet of civilisation, and Ronald Knox was among the most civilised of men. When Aeneas has subdued the native tribes of Italy, he must not only give them walls—he must actually give them manners. Aeneas is to Turnus what Prospero is to Caliban; he secures the white man's supremacy. In the *Iliad* it had not greatly mattered whether Hector or Achilles was the victor, except that most people think Hector was the better man, in the sense that they always thought Bombardier Wells was better—or at any rate more deserving—than the tough who knocked him out. But it wasn't going to change the course of civilisation whether Troy was burnt or remained standing. "The moral of the *Iliad*," said Knox, "is that all this waste of life can happen for the sake of a single paltry woman. In the *Aeneid* the moral is just the opposite, that such tremendous issues can hang on one or two very ordinary lives." The *Aeneid* was an optimistic poem, because the reader knew from the start that the right side was going to come out top in the end. You may object that this was begging the question. But for a Roman of the Augustan age, as for an Englishman of the Elizabethan or the Victorian age, or for a Frenchman of the *grand siècle*, there were some questions that could not be begged—and Rome was one of them.

Ronald Knox would have been the first to appreciate the blessings of the Augustan peace, but of course his deeper preoccupations lay elsewhere, and it was natural that he should turn to Virgil's religious outlook. "What exactly," he asked—as so many have asked—"was the meaning of *pietas?*" He had no difficulty in proving that it did not mean "affectionate" —which was what they had told him it meant at his private school. You had to relate it, first, to the taboos of primitive religion. The woods and mountains were not "peopled by jolly satyrs and desperately respectable nymphs"; they were "full of bogies and goblins." The primitive religion of Rome was largely composed of things that you might not do, and the rationalist might reply that no religion is composed of anything else. Nevertheless a Canon of St. Peter's, or St. Paul's, would have been very disconcerted if you had enumerated for him all the perfectly innocent things that were forbidden to a priest of Jupiter. The last thing that Aeneas asked himself—though whether Virgil asked it is another matter—was whether such and such a thing that had to be done was reasonable. All that mattered was that certain things had to be done in a certain way and at a certain time; and Knox suggested that when we speak of *pius Aeneas*, we

mean, practically speaking, "Aeneas, that trained liturgiolo-
gist" . . . But the meaning of the word could be extended to
include anyone who observed the rules of the game and was
loyal to any natural obligation. Perhaps the best translation
was *conscientious*—because that also explained why Aeneas
was the least bit of a bore. There was no limit to his scruples
—once he had put the sea between himself and Dido. "The
extent of his piety," says Knox, "is enormous. He kills a good
many Rutilians in the *Aeneid*, but he kills far more cattle."
Knox even had the curiosity to go through the poem and
count up Aeneas' bag. He had disposed of fifteen sheep, thirteen bullocks, three bulls, three calves, three pigs, two lambs
and a cow, not to mention five bowls of wine, three of milk,
and three of blood, and various unspecified holocausts. In
fact, so conscientious or scrupulous was Aeneas that one critic
had suggested that he was far more suited to be the founder
of a community of contemplative monks than to be the
founder of an empire. Knox had little acquaintance with contemplative monks at the time he delivered these lectures; but
he replied that it was "much easier to found an empire successfully than to found a successful community of contemplative monks."

Virgilian *pietas*, however, also implied divine reciprocity,
and Aeneas got as good as he gave. His reward was to be in
permanent communication with the gods, with a private line
to Olympus. Virgil had moralised *pietas* into meaning something like divine obligation, and spiritualised it into meaning
something like divine pity. The conception of a covenant between the worshipper and his god had been introduced, and
to this was added the notion of merit. *Dignus* and *mereor*
were among the key-words of the *Aeneid*. From a study of

Virgil's religion Knox was led on to examine his eschatology, and there were two points in which he found this "quite startlingly Christian." One was the Sibyl's account of how a Fairy with a whip extorted confession of their crimes from the souls in Tartarus. It was not everywhere, he said, that you could find a heathen poet expounding the disastrous consequences of dying with unconfessed mortal sin on your conscience. The other point was when Anchises, on meeting Aeneas, congratulates him on his filial obedience in coming down to the shades. Anchises, who was living the life of a beatified saint, had actually witnessed the sufferings of his son and sympathised with them. Knox said that he knew of no other instance in the classics where knowledge of what is going on in the world is attributed to the departed, even to those who have attained Elysium.

In further lectures, Ronald Knox showed how Virgil's belief in destiny still left room for pathos and romantic overtones. The story of Nisus and Euryalus was a witness to his sympathy for the weaker and the defeated side. Knox decribed this sympathy as Christian, and even as democratic. The constant and deliberate use of the word *fuit* aroused our sympathy for a cause irretrievably and tragically lost. It echoed again and again:

nil super imperio moveor; speravimus ista dum Fortuna fuit.

The Trojans could fulfill the injunction of the Epistle to the Hebrews in desiring a better country, but they could never forget for very long the country from which they came—the country that was now no more. The *Aeneid* was an optimistic poem, but it still left room for the regret which belongs to romanticism. The waste of war, the shortness and fragility of human life—these themes were continually stressed; particularly so in the line that always moved Ronald Knox more than any other line in Virgil. Mezentius, already wounded, receives the news that his son Lausus has been killed. Returning to the fight to die, he addresses his horse Rhaebus:

> Rhaebe, diu, res si qua diu mortalibus ulla est,
> viximus.

It was only two years before the Great War would carry off many of Ronald Knox's closest friends; some of them, no doubt, were among the audience that listened to his lectures. Those who knew him in after life often had the impression that *vixi* was at the back of a mind too disciplined to indulge its melancholy; and none could doubt that Virgilian *pietas* was the basis on which the richer pieties of Christian spirituality were slowly and securely built.

In 1959, two years after the death of Ronald Knox, his friend L. E. Eyres collected a number of his papers in a volume entitled *In Three Tongues*. Here are many of his translations into Greek and Latin. They demand a scholarly appraisal which I am incompetent to give; but they demonstrate to the least expert reader his astonishing command of languages which he would have been horrified to hear described as dead. They include passages from Browning, Belloc, Maurice Baring, Lewis Carroll, William Habington and Gerard Manley Hopkins. Some are original compositions: indeed he had inflicted a Latin play on his family while he was still at his private school. When Gervase Elwes, the singer, was killed in an accident during a tour of the United States, Knox sent the following couplet to *The Dublin Review:*

> Ut vocem Deus a terris arcesseret istam,
> Numquid et angelicis defuit una choris.

The visitor to Baghdad may read this inscription on the fountain at the British Embassy:

> Anglia quem mittit siccos bibe vector ad Indos
> Anglia quas praebet, sed Babylonis, aquas.

When the English countryside—and the country-house whither Knox had retreated to work at his translation of the Bible—were filled with urban evacuees at the beginning of the Second World War, the new word found its way into the old language:

> "Eva, cooee" pulsus Paradiso dixit Adamus;
> Echo responsum reddidit "Evacuee."

And when forty of Hilaire Belloc's friends gathered to celebrate his sixtieth birthday, Ronald Knox sent an Horatian Ode for the occasion:

> Sive narraris pedes isse Romam,
> Seu ferox Nonae religasse funem
> Sive mordaci vitiosa plangis
> Saecla flagello.

Here the allusion to Belloc's pilgrimage on foot to Rome, and to his cruises in the *Nona*, will catch the least tutored ear.

Knox was as happy translating from Latin into English as from English into Latin. I had occasion, in a short life of St. Thomas of Canterbury, to quote a poem by the classicist

Hildebert on the ruin of medieval Rome, and I asked Ronald Knox to translate it for me. Since this has not been included in any collection of his papers, I append it here. It shows not only his natural sympathy with the subject, but his mastery of the Alexandrine metre which he was to use to such effect in his satirical verse.

> Rome, that in all-but-ruin hast no peer,
> What once thou wert, the monument is here.
> Age hath thy pride brought low, and sunk in fen
> The shrines of gods, the citadels of men:
> Fallen is the city, needs not that I should
> Write more for epitaph, than *Rome Hath Stood*.
> And yet not Time itself, nor fire, nor foe
> Could all that beauty, all that strength undo:
> A thing so durable man's art did raise
> As heaven's hath idly travailed to efface.
> Get me new wealth, new stones; let Fortune smile
> On sleepless workmen labouring at the pile:
> To match what stands, their effort were in vain,
> Or else what's ruined to restore again:
> Unequalled, what's unchanged, defies their skill,
> And, what lies lost, irreparable still.

3

WHO DUNNITS

HE WROTE five of them, and perhaps he did not take them very seriously; but he wrote them seriously, as he wrote everything else. The purpose, I have always understood, was to supplement the meagre stipend of the Oxford Chaplaincy. He laid down the following rules. The criminal must be someone who has been mentioned in the first five chapters, but he must not be anyone whose thoughts the reader has been allowed to follow. All supernatural or preternatural agencies are ruled out as a matter of course. Not more than one secret room or passage is permissible, and then only in a house where such romantic amenities might be expected to be found. No hitherto undiscovered poisons may be used, nor any scientific device which requires a long explanation for the reader. No Chinaman must figure in the story; no accident must ever aid the detective; nor must he ever have an unaccountable intuition which turns out to be right. The detective must not himself commit the crime, and he is bound to declare any clues upon which he may happen to light. Lastly, the stupid friend of the detective must not conceal from the reader anything which passes through his mind. All these rules Ronald Knox punctiliously obeyed, and he did not fail to point out—in an essay published in *Literary Distractions*— where they had been infringed by others.

The Viaduct Murder (1926) was the first of what might have been a memorable series if sterner counsels and more urgent calls upon his leisure had not dissuaded him. Some men have one detective story in them; E. C. Bentley is a case in point, and here the author was unwise to attempt to rival (even in collaboration) his own masterpiece. Would Ronald Knox have been able, like most writers of detective fiction, to churn them out? Had he that particular ace up his literary sleeve? It is quite possible. But he was handicapped by the lack of a detective. Chesterton had patented Father Brown— and Father Brown would not have been beyond Ronald Knox's invention. He might, of course, have set up a Jesuit in competition; saintly sophistication *versus* saintly simplicity. But that would have given the impression that the regular clergy were getting their own back; and the wider public, to whom such distinctions were meaningless, would have re-sented a Popish plot to capture territory which had the right (they would have said) to sectarian neutrality. With Poirot and Lord Peter Wimsey—another Knoxian possibility—well established in the field, no obvious opening presented itself, although a clergyman of the Established Church would have suited Knox's talents and been a piquant rival to Father Brown. Had Marryat in *The Viaduct Murder* turned out to be the super sleuth instead of the falsely suspected murderer, we might have seen an interesting competition between the Church of England and the Church of Rome—and one which would have left oecumenical relations at least as happy as it found them. But not feeling able, at first, to commit himself to a single detective, Knox did the next best thing—he committed himself to four. They were all amateurs and they were variously competent. Living in the dormy-house adjoining a golf course—the last ignoble transformation of a stately home—they compare notes and speak, like the Fathers of the Oratory, under correction. But whereas most detective stories lead up to a solution of dazzling ingenuity, here the dazzling ingenuity is not in the solution but in the hypothesis. First of all we are invited to believe that the victim and the murderer are one and the same person; and then, upon evidence equally irrefragable, we are asked to suppose that a kindly, if not particularly energetic, clergyman of the Established Church has murdered a parishioner because he disbelieves in the immortality of the soul and publishes his incredulity in the market-place. The surprise of the book is that the one character who has a clear motive for committing the crime does in fact commit it. This is the "dull fact" which gives its title to the concluding chapter. But because we have already been asked to suspect the true murderer and then to avert our suspicions elsewhere, and also because he happens to be a Catholic in good faith, the "dull fact," if it is not quite a sensation, is at least a surprise. It is made clear that a man commits a murder, not because he is or is not a Catholic, but because he is a particular kind of man. Not at all necessarily a bad man—and we are encouraged to believe that this one will make a good end—but a man psychologically conditioned to violence. For this is the second surprise—that a murder which appears to have been premeditated with the utmost refinement of cunning was not premeditated at all. And the third surprise is that although there are four detectives, none of them solves the riddle.

It is a remarkably ingenious story in which it would seem ungenerous to pick holes. But is it very likely that a shady speculator in the City, with an illicit establishment in Chelsea, would preach atheism on the village green? And if there was an elaborate priests' hiding place in your ancestral home, why should you keep quiet about it? People will boast about priests' holes who would never boast about hiding priests; sliding panels are assets anywhere, even in a golf Club. But the book is something more than a diverting and ingenious essay in detection; it is an amiable skit on the Higher Criticism, on the mentality which insists on rejecting *a priori* any explanation which seems likely to be true. If you were proposing to accuse of murder a man with whom you had played several rounds on the golf course, you might feel a certain reluctance to do so to his face. But would you go to the lengths of doing so down a speaking tube? I must confess that this seems to me wildly improbable. Nevertheless Ronald Knox uses the improbability to reinforce his moral—a moral, however, which he charitably invites the reader to skip.

Half the statements which we regard as facts in history and criticism are statements made by critics, which are so ingenious that nobody has the heart to doubt them. And so the silly old world goes on. What if our forefathers are misjudged? We keep our mouths, not our ears, to the metaphone, and the honourable gentlemen get no opportunity to reply: and it doesn't matter much to them, because, like sensible people, they've dropped their end of the tube and left us to talk into empty air.

Ronald Knox had brought to the solution of the *Viaduct Murder* the acuteness of reasoning, the balance of judgment, and a logic which was not the logic of lunacy, that he brought to the solution of much larger mysteries. Those who are interested can watch here a characteristic demonstration of method. His *mise-en-scène* was equally typical. There was "no impatience like that engendered by watching another man look up Bradshaw"—how well he knew it! And where, I cannot help wondering, was his archetypal viaduct? Between Harringworth and Melton Mowbray, almost in sight of the Dominican School at Laxton? Perhaps not; for that one lacked the vital curve—though the curve proved not to be so vital after all. And although Ronald Knox may not have known much about golf, he knew something about golfers:

... twice daily they go round the course, with all the leisurely solemnity of Benedictines reciting their office, and every night they meet in corona to discuss the mysteries of their religion.

In the second of his detective stories, *The Three Taps* (1927), Knox reduces his detectives to two and introduces us to Bredon. To be frank, Bredon is a bore. He would have been better if he had been more like Ronald Knox himself; but the pipe and the pack of Patience cards and the passion for a problem is all they have in common. He hunts in company with his wife Angela—their marital persiflage is rather trying—and with a professional detective, Leyland, whose acumen almost reaches amateur status. He also represents an omnicompetent Insurance Company called The Indescribable which Knox describes with characteristic virtuosity:

The man who is insured with the Indescribable walks the world in armour of proof; those contrary accidents and mortifications which are a source of spiritual profit to the saint, are a source of material advantage to him. No East wind but flatters him with the prospect of a lucrative cold; no dropped banana skin but may suddenly hurl him into affluence. The chicken-farmer whose hen houses are fitted with the Company's auto-matic egg-register can never make a failure of his business. The egg is no sooner laid than it falls gently through a slot, which marks its passage on a kind of taximeter; and if the total of eggs at the end of the month is below the average, the Company pays—I had almost said the Company lays—an exact monetary equivalent for the shortage . . . Wags have made merry at the Company's expense, alleging that a burglar can insure himself against a haul of sham jewels, and a clergyman against insufficient attendance at evensong. They tell stories of a client who murmured "Thank God" as he fell down a lift shaft, and a shipwrecked passenger who manifested the liveliest annoyance at the promptness of his rescuers when he was being paid for floating in a life-belt at the rate of ten pounds a minute.

The mystery concerns the death by gassing of a certain Mr. Mottram, a manufacturer from the Midlands, who likes the Catholic Church without belonging to it. Leyland smells a case of murder and Bredon a case of suicide, and a bet of £40 hangs on the result of their mutual investigations. In the event, neither wins it. The defect of the story is the difficulty of believing in the highly improbable person that Mottram turns out to have been. But it shows Knox's close acquaint-ance with cathedral presbyteries and country pubs. He was as at home with the municipal Gothic of the one as with the bacon and blanc-manges of the other. The contrast is vivid and exact between the pitch-pine panelling on which the previous occupants of the See of Pullford hung in the worst style of ecclesiastical portraiture, with the plaster Madonna which had been successively exiled from the church and the sacristy, and the out-of-tune piano in the living-room of the inn, with its "promiscuous heap of Dissenting hymn-books and forgotten dance tunes reposing on it," and its "picture of Bournemouth in a frame of repulsive shells." Bredon and Leyland between them set the pattern of problems to come; and we realise that they will be solved not only by patience but by Patience.

In *The Footsteps at the Lock* (1928) Ronald Knox moved to territory which he knew as well as any man—the upper reaches of the Thames between Oxford and Cricklade. A great part of the mystery depends upon how far, and how fast, a canoe with a hole in it can float downstream. Ronald Knox was a "river man," and this is the river man's detective story. But he was also, as we have seen, a "railway man," and there is a good deal about catching trains—slow trains, fast trains, London trains, cross-country trains, morning trains, afternoon trains—in *The Footsteps at the Lock*. To Oxford men recurrent references to the 3.12 and the 4.45 will be pleasantly familiar; and indeed the construction of the cipher, the reading of which goes a long way towards the solution of the mystery, is a piece of virtuosity only conceivable in one who knew Bradshaw by heart. *The Footsteps at the Lock*, concerned as it is with the fate (and the redemption) of two particularly unpleasant Oxford men, takes high rank in any anthology of Oxford detective stories; and certain bizarre aspects of the Oxford 'twenties, which must have caused a good deal of trouble to Ronald Knox in the early years of his Chaplaincy, are strongly, though discreetly, stressed. For his detective he goes back to Bredon. Here, again, the trouble is that Bredon is not very interesting, and the book suffers from a lack of mastery at the centre. You know that Bredon will read the riddle, but you do not feel it. You take it on trust because, in the world of W. H. Smith & Son,[1] a detective who fails to detect is a contradiction in terms. Bredon's wife is not very interesting either, and neither is Leyland, who bats doggedly for the Yard. One misses the foursome from *The Viaduct Murder;* only Mr. Carmichael makes a disappointingly fleeting appearance. The greatest detective stories— *Trent's Last Case* is the classic example—combine stunning surprise with pellucid simplicity. *The Footsteps at the Lock* is just a shade too complicated; too many clues are left lying about on the river banks; and the book becomes, in places, a little tiring to read—like an *impasse* in a crossword puzzle.

Detective stories may be divided into two kinds; those whose interest lies exclusively in the solution of a problem, and those which charm us by their atmosphere, intrigue us by their psychology, and even point us, not too obtrusively, to great moral truths. *The Footsteps at the Lock* is of this second kind. It hardly pretends to psychological depth; but it does show the workings of the natural moral law in one who imagined himself to be unnaturally immoral—and it does this without any forcing of the character in question. But the book takes one back beyond its personalities and its problems to the Oxford of *The Scholar Gypsy*—to an ideal, a Platonic Oxford, which Ronald Knox represented as well as any man then living. How many friends of his—men of his own generation and men of a much younger generation now placed in his spiritual care—must have seen him, in semi-laicised recreational attire, white shirt and black trousers, guiding his punt

[1] The well-known firm of British newsagents and circulating libraries.

or paddling his canoe down the Cherwell in the late summer afternoon; and how poignantly the memory must come back to them when they read such a passage as this:

The river lay infinitely beautiful, windless under a cloudless sky. The tiniest fidgeting motion of your body pencilled fresh ripples on the cool surface of the stream. The red earth of the banks, and the green fringe that surmounted them, showed in mellow contrast under the equable light of evening. The reeds stood straight and motionless as sentinels, just fringed with a distant horizon of tree-tops. The splashing of cows in the shallows, the churning of far-off reaping machines, the cries of children, punctuated the stillness with companionship. Mint and meadow-sweet and lying hay blended their scents with intolerable sweetness in that most delicate of all mediums, the smell of clean river-water. The stream, now dazzling in the sunlight, now mysterious and dark under the tree shadows, seemed to conspire with the easy strokes of the paddle. Nature had determined, it appeared, to forget the tragedy and go on as if nothing had happened.

The fourth of Ronald Knox's detective stories—*The Body in the Silo* (1933)[2] is the best and most ingenious of the five. The scene is Herefordshire—not his usual beat, but no doubt a visit to Belmont Abbey had taught him its character and topography:

Sudden, conical hills thickly wooded, old grey archways that had once been lodge gates, pointing along grass-grown roads up avenues now meaningless, farmhouses older and more substantial than is our English wont, vistas, as you climbed a hill, of hops

[2] New York: Macmillan, 1959.

stretching across the fields, row upon row, like Venetian blinds; orchards of whitened trunks and fruit-laden boughs, little brick and timber villages huddling round duckponds, tall hedges with white-faced cows at the gaps in them looking at you with an outraged expression, as if they suspected you of being after the door-scraper. . . .

Through this lush countryside runs the river Wye; a secluded river, to be sure, but is there any other writer of detective fiction to whom it would have whispered: *secretum meum mihi?* And on its banks stands the Puginesque mansion where the guests are gathered for a house party which seems curiously to lack a *raison d'être*. Indeed, it is this which first sets Bredon sniffing. Wit crackles among the tea-cups: "It isn't that I mind tennis, but it hasn't got the tradition value of cricket. Who ever heard of somebody refusing to do a shady thing on the ground that it wasn't tennis?" "I think it's such a pity to be rough without being a diamond, don't you?" It is shrewdly observed that ninety per cent of brilliant academic careers lead to nothing; and that one of the main differences between England and Scotland is that in England biography is the key to geography, whereas in Scotland it's the other way about. There is nothing original about the wrong man being suspected—Ronald Knox never showed disrespect for the conventions—but the originality of the story lies in the wrong man being murdered. When the solution of the puzzle comes to Bredon over a game of Patience, his features—never very clearly definable—dissolve, and it is Ronald Knox himself whom we see, pipe in mouth, bent over the cards in the long sitting-room at the Old Palace. A knock comes at the door; perhaps an unknown undergraduate wants to hear about the Catholic Church. The pipe is laid down and the game of Patience—like the *roman policier* itself—is set aside for larger matters.

In *Still Dead* (1934) Bredon does not play Patience, and a long country walk—another of Ronald Knox's favorite recreations—helps him to clear up the mystery of how the same dead body came to be found in the same place at the same time of day twice within a space of forty-eight hours, and almost, but not quite, in the same position. Here the move has been to Scotland, and one guesses the book may well have been written during a Long Vacation, when Ronald Knox was the guest of Mrs. Stirling at Keir. The neighbourhood of Perth and Gleneagles clearly indicates what the Railways invariably describe as the Gateway to the Highlands. The solution is both ingenious and plausible, and the characterization, even when it is crude, is amusing. Ronald Knox knew all about retired majors who equate Ireland and India in a blanket condemnation of sedition; I have myself heard a member of the Anglo-Irish Protestant ascendency remark, as the servant left the luncheon table: "This country is so like India." And he knew that a certain type of well-preserved lady in tweeds never says "pretty," but "prooty." By 1934 the Oxford groups were adding to the embarrassments of the Oxford Chaplaincy, and when the ailing laird asks for "guidance" and a member of what are called the "Circles" descends upon the baronial Neo-Gothic of Dorn, there is no mistaking the allusion.

4

SATIRE AND FANTASY

THE HUMORIST IS OUT to make a lot of people laugh; the
satirist is out to make certain people squirm. In doing the
second a writer may incidentally do the first, but the laughter
he excites will have a satirical sting. Mr. Evelyn Waugh, for
example, is both incidentally and exorbitantly funny. Everyone acknowledged Ronald Knox to be a wit, but nobody
dreamt of describing him as a clown—and the clown is the
purest, because he is the most gratuitous, of comedians. As
Knox pointed out in his introduction to *Essays in Satire*
(1928), wit is "first and last a matter of expression . . . You
cannot think a witty thought, even, without thinking in
words. But humour can be wordless; there are thoughts that
lie too deep for laughter itself." He was not concerned, however, to distinguish between humour and wit, but to draw the
more delicate and difficult distinction between humour and
satire. He did not know how many people his own satire
made to squirm, because they were unlikely to have told him;
but he must have realised, over the years, how many it made
to laugh.

Humour, in Knox's summary, was concerned with man and the unexpected. A drunkard was funny, because you expected him to be sober; a madman because you expected him to be sane; a foreigner because you expected him to be English; and a man falling down because you expected him to be standing up. Humour, divorced from satire, was a largely modern phenomenon. To Burke it did not appear consistent "with an age of true politeness." Struggling to birth in Jane Austen, it reached maturity in Dickens and Calverley. Knox also noted that humour, divorced from satire, belonged to the English-speaking races alone, whereas satire was international. Humour sought identity with the victim; it ran with the hare whereas the satirist hunted with the hounds. Its operation was more secret and its disclosures more mysterious than the operations and disclosures of satire; but it was the property of a particular age and civilisation. Satire was of all ages and of every civilisation; "a normal function of the human genius" and a permanent category of literature. Humour appeared and disappeared, more capriciously than poetry itself. Knox might have added that you spoke of so-and-so's sense of humour, as if it were a personal characteristic, or even a personal charisma. Some people had it, and some people had it not, and no two had it in quite the same way. It was a sort of psychological handwriting. But you never refer to so-and-so's sense of satire.

The great difference was that satire had a specific and deadly intention. For anyone who realised that it was aimed at him, it could have "an intensely remedial effect," purifying the "spiritual system of man as nothing else that is human can possibly do." That was why every young man in love should read *The Egoist:*

In a word, humour without satire is, strictly speaking, a perversion, the misuse of a sense. Laughter is a deadly explosive which was meant to be wrapped up in the cartridge of satire, and so, aimed unerringly at the appointed target, deal its salutary wound; humour without satire is a flash in the pan; it may be pretty to look at, but it is, in truth, a waste of ammunition. Or, if you will, humour is satire that has run to seed; trained no longer by an artificial process, it has lost the virility of its stock. It is port from the wood, without the depth and mystery of its vintage rivals. It is a burning-glass that has lost its focus; a passenger, pulling no weight in the upstream journey of life; meat that has had the vitamins boiled out of it; a clock without hands. The humorist, in short, is a satirist out of a job; he does not fit into the scheme of things; the world passes him by.

It is a fine example of Knox's high-spirited, debating prose, suggesting one of his virtuoso performances at the Oxford Union; and he concludes the essay by admitting a certain doubt as to whether there is any truth in the views he has put forward. "But I do not see that there can be any harm in having said what I thought, even if I am no longer certain that I think it." He had not failed to notice that the reputation of contemporary humorists rather rapidly declined; for his own part, he would only guarantee the immortality of Max Beerbohm, because Max Beerbohm was really a satirist in humorist's clothing. The rewards of the humorist are like the rewards of other public entertainers; they are very handsome while they last. The pure humour of P. G. Wodehouse earned its thousands, while the pure satire of Belloc's political novels barely earned their advances. But Ronald Knox need not have worried, for it is upon his output—very small—of satirical writings that his reputation with the common reader, unprejudiced by any religious commitment, so very largely rests.

Knox did not invent a new form of satire, unless we except his broadcast on the British Revolution, which was less a satire than a squib. The old forms which he inherited from Dryden and Swift served his purpose admirably. Already, at Eton, he was committing jaundiced epigrams to a private note-book; but then it was easy, he tells us, "to be a Schopenhauer at thirteen." Like nearly all satirists, Knox was a conservative in the sense that he was out to mock the insolent pretensions of modernity. It was not that all old things were good, but that certain new things were silly. Most of these essays, however varied their subject matter, are satires either on the Higher Criticism or the Lower Morality. The higher criticism of the Bible amused without disturbing him, but the notion that the *Iliad* was written by a committee roused him to fury, and he exposed it by applying the same method to the Sherlock Holmes stories. In *Absolute and Abitofhell* he is picking up some loose stones, and slinging them at the authors of *Foundations*. This is at once a parody and a pastiche, but it is more seriously intentioned than either of these literary genres generally manages to be. It is the *cleverest* thing that Ronald Knox ever wrote. The distinguished Oxford theologians still wear their black eyes like certificates of immortality; and Knox even included one or two who had not so directly asked for them. He did not spare Dr. J. M. Thompson of Magdalen:

> Say, why did Magdala, renown'd in Ships,
> Withhold the Tribute of *his* dauntless Lips,
> Who, setting out the Gospel Truths t' explain,
> Thought all that was not German, not germane:

nor Dr. Hastings Rashdall of New College:

> Why did Neapolis, aloof like Asher,
> Withhold—the Name is in the Book of Jasher—
> Where, 'mid the thunders of a boisterous Quad,
> He ponders on the Raison d'Etre of God.

For the rest, let us call the roll. The first victim, William Temple, was a Balliol man, but he had deserted Balliol for the Headmastership of Repton and the incumbency of St. James's, Piccadilly:

> A man so broad, to some he seem'd to be
> Not one, but all mankind in effigy.

Temple's sympathies were as broad as his theology and his physique:

> "Not from the few, the learned and the pale"
> —So ran his message—"we expect our Sale;
> Man in the Street, our Publication con—
> What matter if the Street be Askkelon?"

and so to Canon Streeter:

> Himself believing as believing went
> In that wild Heyday of th' Establishment,
> When, on his throne at Lambeth, Solomon
> Uneasy murmur'd, "Something must be done."
> When suave politeness, temp'ring bigot Zeal,
> Corrected "I believe" to "One does feel";

and Nevile Talbot, later Archbishop of Pretoria:

> In Height magnificent, in Depth profound,
> Bless'd with more sense than some, than all more sound;

and Rawlinson, afterwards Bishop of Derby, with whom Knox had walked along the electric railway line between Blackpool and Rossall, learning the facts of Modernism:

> Who cried, as joyfully he bound his sheaves,
> "What I believe is what the Church believes":
> Yet some might find it matter for Research,
> Whether the Church taught him, or he the Church.

The last to be pilloried were Richard Brook of Merton and Walter Moberley of Lincoln. Moberley had written a book on Punishment, still regarded as a classic by students of delinquency; as Dean of Lincoln and Proctor of the University, he had brought an imposing presence, an inflexible will, and a philosophic temper to the problems of keeping undergraduates from climbing over College walls:

> His views on Punishment what need to tell?
> Poor, proctor'd Victims lately knew them well,
> His pregnant Logick filled their only Want,
> Temp'ring EZECHIEL with a Dash of KANT.

The poem was not an answer to *Foundations*, but a good-humoured anticipation of it. The two issues of the *Oxford Magazine* in which it first appeared were sold out within a few days of publication.

Reunion All Round must not be read as a tilt against oecumenism, but as a warning against that blurring of distinctions which makes any kind of reunion impossible. It was provoked by the conference at Kikiyu in East Africa, at which representatives of the Anglican dioceses of Uganda and Mombasa agreed with the representatives of various Free Church missions on a programme of co-operation recognizing, among other things, an exchange of pulpits and the admission of non-Anglicans to Communion in Anglican churches. In the Church of the future Knox, now modelling himself on Swift, imagines Mohammedans and Christians in easy accord, ruled by a combined Hierarchy of Archbishops, Pashas (corresponding to Bishops), Archdeacons, Mullahs (corresponding to Rural Deans), Incumbents, and Hadjis (corresponding to Unbeneficed Clergy). The Pope would be allowed "to take rank as a retired Missionary Bishop, thus leaving him the Insignia of Power without any Sphere in which to exercise, or Income with which to abuse it. The Cardinals would disperse among the Common-Rooms of Oxford and Cambridge, where they could exercise to the full their Talent for Intrigue without having any serious effect, for good or ill, upon the Destinies of the Nation." The only test of orthodoxy would be an oath of unfeigned disbelief in all the Scriptures of the Old and New Testament; and within a century the Church of England might illustrate her Catholic vocation by including "within her Borders every possible Shade of Belief, Quod umquam, quod usquam, quod ab ullis."

This was hard hitting, and Ronald Knox would perhaps have written a little differently on the eve of the Second Vatican Council. But in 1928 a great many people thought that dogma was the dark cloud on the horizon of universal brotherhood, and that if nobody believed anything in particular, everybody would love their neighbour as themselves. It is interesting to note that whereas *Absolute and Abitofhell* had been the work of months, *Reunion All Round* was completed in four days. Knox, who was staying in a country-house for a reading party, found himself prowling round the shelves of the library while the other guests were finishing a game of billiards. Here he renewed acquaintance with Swift, and the idea of using the style of Swift to ridicule the logical corollary to Kikiyu took hold upon his mind. The pamphlet had a considerable sale and was read aloud to the Prime Minister, Mr. Asquith, as he sat in his bathing costume on the banks of the Thames during one of the hottest summers on record. Its argument might be a *reductio ad absurdum*, but no satire was ever more seriously intended. If the principles of Kikiyu were right, something very like an *omnium gatherum* of Christians and atheists in a church based on fundamental disagreement was well within the limits of fantasy, and might hardly be beyond the boundaries of fact.

A New Cure for Religion went closer to the mark than Ronald Knox may have intended, for it does look as if some people are more naturally conditioned to believe than others; and Dr. Mahu's proposal to extirpate or introduce the religious gland, at the patient's choice, invites the question why Grace has a harder time with Dick than with Harry. It also invited the objection of Mr. Clump—that the total extirpation of religious feeling would rob our unlawful pleasures of a great part of their pleasurableness. But Dr. Mahu claimed that the abolition of hypocrisy would be assured when the sincerity of a man's religious profession could be tested by radiographical inspection; and that the problem of Christian reunion would be solved, once for all, when every English Christian was "englanded" with a single gland of fellowship. *The New Sin* was in fact the old sin—the primal vice of curiosity. When the Albert Hall or the Harringay Arena—so to speak—is packed to hear Professor Laileb expound his recipe, he disappears in a flash—was it the flash of a Fleet Street camera?—and leaves his audience to their fury, their frustration, and their frenzied pursuit of these hackneyed sins, which sickened them but which they could not do without.

In the next essay Knox applies the methods of the Higher Criticism to Sherlock Holmes. The evil that he did—notably the dirty and deleterious habit of taking cocaine—lived after him; the good was interred with him in the Reichenbach. Serious inconsistencies are pointed out. Why is John H. Watson, M.D., addressed by his wife as James? Were there— as Baenecke maintained—two Watsons; a proto-Watson who wrote *The Adventures, The Sign of Four, The Hound of the Baskervilles*, and most of the *Memoirs*, and a deutero-Watson who wrote *The Study in Scarlet, The Gloria Scott*, and *The Return?* It all hinged on whether you regarded *The Final Problem* as genuine. If it was genuine, then the stories in *The Return* were fabrications, and Baenecke marshalled the evidence against them by showing significant changes in the character and methods of Holmes; impossibilities in the story itself; and inconsistencies with the previous narrative. Thus the true Holmes was never discourteous to a client, but the Holmes of the *Adventure of the Three Students* "shrugged his shoulders in ungracious acquiescence while our visitor . . . poured forth his story." The true Holmes never splits an in-finitive; the Holmes of the *Return* splits at least three. Was it likely that a University scholarship paper should be printed only one day before the examination, and that it should consist of only half a chapter of Thucydides? How came it that the dummy placed in the Baker Street window should be draped in "the old mouse-coloured dressing-gown," when it was in a *blue* dressing-gown that Holmes had smoked an ounce of shag tobacco at a sitting, while he unravelled the mystery of the *Man with the Twisted Lip?* For Sauwosch this was conclusive. "This is not the first time that a coat of many colours has been as a deception used! But in truth Sherlock, our modern Joseph, has altogether disappeared, and the evil beast Watson has him devoured."

Knox does not support the theory of two Watsons, but he professes to believe that there were two cycles of stories—one that actually happened, and one that Watson invented. Knox is very good on Watson: like the Chorus in a Greek tragedy, he "is ever in touch with the main action, and seems to share the full privileges of the audience; yet, like the Chorus, he is always about three stages behind the audience in the unravelling of the plot." Knox goes very thoroughly into the question of Holmes' education. His scientific training would point to Cambridge, but then he confesses to no acquaintance with the scenery of Cambridgeshire. True, he was a natural recluse, but however resolutely he sported his oak[1]—one feels inclined to add—so observant a man could hardly have refrained from looking out of the window of his railway carriage somewhere between Cambridge and Audley End. Indeed it was doubtful if he had read science at all, since he had only spent two years at the University. So Knox concluded that Holmes had been to Oxford, probably at the

[1] The outer door of a student's rooms at Oxford, which he shuts to protect his privacy. To "sport" an "oak" is to shut it.

"House." It was unlikely that he had read Greats, although his knowledge of philosophy and literature was wider than Watson had at first suspected. We know that he was ready with an apt quotation from Tacitus, Goethe, Flaubert and Thoreau, and that he was seen to be reading Petrarch in a carriage of the Great Western Railway. It was possible—although Knox refrained from suggesting it—that he had come down without taking a degree. It was even conceivable that he had been sent down, since his athletic prowess and his latent curiosity about the workings of the criminal mind would both have fitted him for the scaling of College walls.

Knox answers most of the questions that the addict is likely to ask about Watson and Sherlock Holmes, and there is not much left of the Higher Criticism by the time he has done so, and has proceeded further to investigate the identity of the Pseudo-Bunyan, the authorship of *In Memoriam*—was it Queen Victoria?—and the vexed question of whether the Life of Johnson and the Hebridean Journal were by the same hand. Yet on one small point he leaves my curiosity unsatisfied. Is he quite certain that the Calais boat train stopped at Canterbury, even in the heyday of the South Eastern and Chatham? And by what circuitous route did Holmes and Watson reach the Continent? The Newhaven-Dieppe crossing was not yet in operation. Everything points, therefore, to Southampton-Havre—via Ashford, Rye, Hastings, Brighton and Portsmouth. It must, in those days, have been a long cross-country journey; and one would like to know whether they spent the night, since they were very deliberately in no hurry, at the Royal Albion or the Old Ship. But I am not quite sure even about Southampton-Havre; my Bradshaw is not sufficiently out of date.

Memoirs of the Future (1923) purports to have been written by Opal, Lady Porstock, in 1988—which suggests that it might just as well have been written in 1984, and that in turn provokes comparisons. If Ronald Knox had composed his prediction at the same time as George Orwell's, it might have cut more savagely. But here Knox was out to amuse, where Orwell was out to warn and to instruct. The book belongs to fantasy rather than to satire, and it will only amuse those who are interested in, and acquainted with, the doings of the leisured classes. Dedicated to, among others, his brother E. V. Knox, it might have brightened the pre-Muggeridge *Punch*. It was a *jeu d'esprit* which would have appealed only to those who were still living fairly comfortably; it was calculated to excite neither tears nor terror. There are some shrewd guesses —that the "commonwealth of Czecho-Slovakia" would be short-lived and that the railway companies would no longer be privately owned; others, more extravagant, that Rugby Football would be played in girls' schools, that the young things would be sitting down to their numismatics class as early as 10.30 a.m., and that their star goal-keeper would end up as the Captain of a P.&O. liner. Ronald Knox was needlessly pessimistic in imagining that English tea would be habitually "laced" with stronger beverages; he would have been safer in predicting that tea is the one thing in England which quite certainly will never change. Well-meaning attempts to emulate it overseas are the only surviving threat to Anglo-American relations.

Opal, Lady Porstock, had seen the foundation of some plausible new Oxford societies—the Curzon, the Asquith; but it was never remotely on the cards that the Oxford University Dramatic Society, profoundly transformed as it has become, would have produced an entertainment called "Oh, blast it all"—even in the Lent of 1936. It was, on the other hand, only too likely that, three years later, non-stop performances of the "Ring" should have been given at Bayreuth —and the prophecy was made before Hitler was ever heard of. Now and again, a more serious, a wistful note is struck. The following is a very accurate intuition of later middle age:

. . . the moment when one drops out of the movement that goes on in one's generation: it is just like dropping out of a competition, the same mixture of disappointment and relief. You will find that you have suddenly stood still, when you had no idea that you had been moving, like getting off one of those murderous moving platforms when you're not thinking. You will have turned from a competitor in life into a spectator, and your first thought will be that everything round you changes, and changes very rapidly.

Ronald Knox was still a comparatively young man when he looked into the future, and there was nothing in the prospect that pleased him. He realised already that he was out of tune with the modern world. In only one respect was he wildly optimistic; he imagined that doctors would be paid according to their results and not according to their endeavours. Otherwise the future—up to date—has bettered his ghastliest predictions, and when he at last came to terms with its ghastliness, the situation was far too serious for fantasy, and he met it not with satire but compassion.

5

FROM THE OLD PALACE
FIRESIDE

I SOMETIMES IMAGINE myself being asked by a stranger or a foreigner—one of my American friends, perhaps—in which book of Ronald Knox's they will find the fullest flavour of his personality. "Yes," I fancy them saying, "we know that he was a fine preacher, a skilled writer of detective stories, a brilliant scholar and all the rest of it. We know that he wrote the story of his conversion. But if you who knew him wanted to introduce him to us who did not, which of his books would you choose to effect the introduction?" A difficult question; and I might reply by asking what sort of an introduction was required. "We don't want to hear him preach," comes the hypothetical answer, "we don't want him to hear our confessions, we don't want to argue with him, but we do want to hear him talk—on as many subjects as possible, including himself." The request is not unreasonable, and I think I should have to point my friend to *Literary Distractions* (1958), a collection of posthumous gleanings which don't in the least suggest that there has been any scraping of the barrel.

You might have supposed that Ronald Knox would have broadcast now and then, and perhaps have wondered why he had not done so more frequently. He may have had his doubts about the B.B.C, but it never occurred to him that it had not come to stay. The last subject, however, on which you would have imagined him broadcasting was Birmingham. Somehow you did not connect him with Birmingham, any more than you connected him with Manchester—until you remembered that his father had been the Bishop of that highly industrialised see. Mr. Evelyn Waugh's biography would have put you right on both points, but I am supposing *per impossible* that you have not read Mr. Waugh's biography. The red bricks of the one city and the black bricks of the other do not meet your preconceptions of Ronald Knox; you associate him, rather, with mellow or with flaking stone. Yet here he is telling us over the air that from the age of four to the age of fifteen Birmingham was all that was meant by home; and that as he approaches Snow Hill by the railway, "the dingy brick arcading that faces the embankment still evokes, by the very sight of it, an illusory lightness of the heart"—because it meant coming home for the holidays. For his father had been Vicar of Aston before becoming Bishop of Manchester. Ronald Knox was a son of the manse; he was not born into the episcopal or any other kind of purple, though he grew up into it and acquired, eventually, a purple of his own. You would not, either, have associated him with Association Football; yet here he is proclaiming his loyalty to Aston Villa, and remembering "the panic of the human squeeze" when he was swept out, or in, through the gates of the arena. You did, perhaps, associate him with the Birmingham Oratory; but of the Oratory, in those days, he knew nothing. Now, as he looked back, he confessed that he himself had probably changed more radically than Birmingham. "Could I really boo a referee nowadays? Could I still feel enthusiastic about the stuffed lion?" (a popular inmate of the museum). "It is a dreadful confession, but I feel as if it must be I, not Birmingham, that has changed."

Ronald Knox was a man of intellectual, as distinct from animal, high spirits. He would set the table on a roar with a kind of drooping diffidence. You might wonder, for instance, how a man who crossed the Channel with such distaste should have felt himself sufficiently at home in French to translate the Autobiography of Ste. Thérèse of Lisieux; and if you want to recover the gaiety of one of those gatherings which he enlivened with a legendary brilliance, you cannot do better than read *French with Tears*. The punctuating laughter positively reverberates from the printed page. Ronald Knox succeeds in being funny about the French, but even funnier about his own incapacity to converse with them. Although he never had a French governess, he learnt French at an early age and shed his first tears over the wanton irregularity of *bouillir*. Then came the school-books with their unbelievable sentences—"donnez-moi la plume, l'encre et le papier du jardinier"—unbelievable because no people were less interested in gardening than the French, and none whose paper was more vile, ink more watery and pens more scratchy; and the schoolmasters, Mr. Evans *alias* "Bam," M. Cuvelier *alias* "Cow-belly," and M. Hua who was reputed to enter Windsor Castle by a secret door after dark for the purpose of telling dirty stories to King Edward VII.

Ronald Knox—to be serious for a moment—not only believed the peace of the world depended on the Anglo-French alliance, but he maintained that French was infinitely the best language for spiritual reading. Bremond was as entertaining as a novel, although Knox did not read French novels. "French has such a curious way of making things look indelicate even when they're really quite all right." It was not so long since a Belgian publishing house, catering for a specially Catholic public, had produced a translation of *The Body in the Silo* where the chapter heading *An Eloping Race* appeared as *La Chasse au Ravisseur*. The book had been seen through the press by a Jesuit, but that did not prevent Ronald Knox from wondering whether the relatively innocent words might not have been translated differently. As for his tongue-tied reluctance to converse in French, that was really a distaste for doing anything badly on the part of one who did nearly everything so well; a prizewinner's *pudeur*, and the self-consciousness of a race on whose dominions, in those happy days, the sun never dreamt of setting. A picture of Ronald Knox faintly responding "Parfaitement" to an enthusiastic French visitor anxious to recruit the *jeunesse Catholique* of Oxford for some vague Continental *ralliement* would be a priceless addition to contemporary caricature. Such a picture would make us laugh, to be sure; but it would also tell us a world of truth about the difficulties of Anglo-French relations.

French with Tears is one of the most amusing essays in the English language, and I should not be surprised if it found its way into some future anthology when weightier works by Ronald Knox have long remained on the shelves. It sparkles with so apparently effortless a spontaneity that the unwary reader may be tempted to suppose that he just "threw it off." Never believe it. You may bet your last dime that he polished it as smoothly as anything destined for the pulpit of West-minster Cathedral. One or two of the sparks might have found their way into his conversation, but Ronald Knox would have disappointed you if you imagined he was what is generally understood by a "brilliant talker." Better that he should go on talking to you through these occasional papers, none of which were published in his lifetime. You may gen-erally know a man by the books he reads as well as by the books he writes, and here Ronald Knox left us a number of valuable clues. He was not a professional literary critic, though he might well have been one if more important work had not claimed him.

From the day when he read *The Man Who Was Thursday* as an undergraduate, Chesterton influenced him more than any other of his near-contemporaries. Chesterton's paradoxes had become the platitudes of Knox's thought. How, he asked, as he sat down to look once again at Chesterton's romances, was a man who had made "Chesterton his hero any time these last thirty years to turn himself upside down and see Ches-terton not as something taken for granted"? He had once compared *The Man Who Was Thursday* to *The Pilgrim's Progress* rewritten in the style of *The Pickwick Papers;* now he identified Innocent Smith with Chesterton himself, and compared his effect on the boarding-house with the effect of The Stranger in *The Passing of the Third Floor Back.* He also observed that Chesterton had never found it in his chival-rous heart to create a really dislikeable woman. As a fellow-member of the Detective Club, Knox was naturally interested in the Father Brown stories, for Chesterton had succeeded just where Knox had failed—in creating a memorable detec-tive. It was all the luck of having met Monsignor John

O'Connor at the right moment—when you wanted to be received into the Catholic Church. But Knox doubted whether
the Father Brown stories, for all their popularity, were as
influential with the post-1918 generation of readers as the
earlier romances had been with his own contemporaries. For
one thing, Chesterton's philosophy had either been digested
or found unacceptable; and for another thing, readers were so
interested in watching Father Brown plucking out the heart
of the problem that they were indifferent to the deeper mysteries he disclosed in doing so. Knox even admitted that in the
later stories the didactic purpose overshadowed the detective
interest.

From Chesterton it was an easy step to Belloc, to whose
literary genius and method Ronald Knox's own talents were
more akin. He had set *The Path to Rome* as a holiday task to
his form at Shrewsbury, and composed an index for it under
more than three hundred heads. How acute to have seen that
where Belloc had written like an old man in his youth,
Chesterton had written like a boy even in his late maturity!
He thought—again how rightly—that *Emmanuel Burden* was
one of the greatest satires in English literature, although he
noted how Belloc, in the last memorable pages of that book,
dropped the mask of satire altogether. "He was too many-
sided a man to put only a part of himself into anything he
wrote." He was too versatile to be labelled; "in letters, as in
life, the severity of his lips is pulled downwards, all of a sudden, into a smile." It would be difficult for the Professors of
the future to discuss the serious achievements in the sonnet
form of a man who was capable of the following opening
line—

Would that I had £300,000.

Knox accurately placed Belloc in the lineage of Milton, Dryden and Gray; he was a poet who held that the first business of poetry was to be verse.

Rather more unexpected was Knox's appreciation of Crashaw. Here we may be disposed to argue—not about Crashaw's gifts, but about Knox's slight disparagement of the other, and surely greater, Metaphysicals. Can we really admit that Donne was not "fundamentally, a religious man"? Are not "Batter my heart, three-personed God" and the *Hymn to God the Father* as religious as Hopkins? We may allow that Donne was sexually obsessed, and Ronald Knox was nervous to admit the necessity of obsession to much great literature; but surely Donne's tormented sense of sin was the mark of a deeply religious temperament? Also, some of us will be up in arms at the suggestion that Herbert was no more than a "moderate poet." Minor, in the technical sense, perhaps; but "moderate" suggests a plain Beta, and surely Herbert deserves better than that? Knox is on safer ground when he hazards the opinion that when people have given up reading the classics altogether, they will find it difficult to understand "the nature or the inspiration of Jacobean poetry." He himself understood the debt of Crashaw to Ovid because he had translated the *Invitation to the Countess of Denbigh* into elegiacs only a few days before he accepted a similar invitation and was himself received into the Catholic Church. Is there a professional literary critic who could say as much? "You do not really understand a poem until you have translated it into Latin verse"—which is a little hard on the rest of us.

Ronald Knox was a devoted novel-reader, by which I mean

that he re-read a limited number of novels very frequently. "Among all the detestable habits which make me angry with my contemporaries, and still more with my juniors, I know none worse than this; their habit of inventing new art-forms which make you ashamed of admiring the old." He was defending Robert Louis Stevenson, a firm favourite ever since he had run about the school-room chanting "Yo-ho-ho and a bottle of rum." In later years he returned constantly to *The Wrecker*. He saw that the battle in Stevenson was more often than not between good and evil, rather than between right and wrong; it was a metaphysical and not an ethical combat. After all, it was Stevenson who had made an optimist of Chesterton, and that was something to be thankful for. Also, Knox expected a novelist to tell a story, and here Trollope, in spite of his "utility" prose, was as readable as Stevenson. Knox lived to see Trollope return to fashion, but that did not impress him. He knew every corner of Barsetshire long before it had been rediscovered—just as he had learnt the Ingoldsby Legends sprawling on a hearth-rug in the nursery—and he saluted the magic by which Trollope, alone among English novelists, had enriched England with a forty-first county. He also noticed that however felicitous Trollope had been in portraying the clergy, he had been even more felicitous in portraying their wives. Trollope, like Jane Austen, was his idea of a novelist. He told a story and created characters: he didn't merely lead you on from one bedroom to another on the grounds that he was being psychological, or from one place to another on the grounds that he was being picaresque. Trollope stayed where he was—not necessarily in the same spot, but at least in the same diocese.

Sir Arnold Lunn, in his valuable reminiscences of Ronald

Knox,[1] observes that Knox was not a very willing "co-operator" with the Church of England. I have already suggested the same thing. He had been more concerned, in his own Aeneid, with the weaknesses of the Church of England than with its strength. But he remained attached to it when he could put it, so to speak, on ice. *Barchester Pilgrimage* (1936) gave him his opportunity. The book assumed that a sufficiency of readers were as well acquainted with Trollope as he was, and Maurice Baring, to whom it was dedicated, reminded him, when it was three parts written, that practically no one would read it because practically no one had ever heard of Barchester. He might have added, with all respect to Knox, that they would want to hear what Trollope had said about it first. So Knox crossed his Ts in a dedicatory preface, realising that "to be an ass in a lion's skin is dangerous work at the best of times, but you look even more of an ass if you are meeting people who have never heard of the lion." The simile was not very apt, since no novelist is less leonine than Trollope, and even Ronald Knox hesitated to class him with the Immortals. But he remained the representative Victorian novelist and Knox had come into the world trailing quite a few clouds of that particular glory.

The book is an immensely skillful pastiche, and entertaining even for those readers with a limited curiosity about what goes on in the Cathedral Close. It will induce you to take an early train to Barchester, if you have not been there for some time, or even if, by some literary oversight, you have never been there at all. We follow the heart-beats of Johnny Bold, the Warden's grandson, and the uncertain vocation of Marmaduke Thorne, grandson to the Prebendary. Here the new

[1] See *And Ever New.*

Catholic church—"down by the station"—casts its competing shadow over the certitudes of the Close; over the "tall, stuffed hassocks, and Tallis in F, and the pleasant smell of musty old prayer-books." There is some competition, too, when the doubtful centenary of St. Ewold comes to be celebrated; and the face-lift of the cathedral itself, with more ritual and less dogma, is nicely registered. The Warden's hospital is turned into a flourishing public school, from which the headmaster resigns because he doubts whether the public schools have any further utility, just as he is on the point of being asked to do so because he has married a *divorcée*. Throughout the book, the ageing verger, Mr. Bunce, acts as a *laudator temporis acti. Barchester Pilgrimage* is none the less enjoyable because Mr. John Betjeman is probably the only man alive who will enjoy it to the full—and probably regrets that he did not write it.

One wishes that Ronald Knox had written about Jane Austen, but he was reading her, once again, in the very last weeks of his life when he was incapable of reading anything else. That is one of the biggest compliments that has ever been paid to Jane Austen, and one would like to think she knows it. There is another novelist about whom Knox wrote no word, although he must have known him—Walter Scott. In the autumn of 1957 he had been invited to propose the toast at the Scott dinner in Edinburgh, but he had already received another invitation which he was powerless to refuse—for death does not take no for an answer. In a life so wonderfully and variously fulfilled one hardly likes to speak of omissions —but this is one of the very few things that Ronald Knox was unable to do which many of us would like him to have done. For nobody could have done it so well.

He was not, as I have said, a travelled man; but, for all that, it was a lecture he gave to his fellow-passengers on an Hellenic cruise which lets in a little light on his love and knowledge of the classics. What should he talk about? He had not spoken much on the classics since he had lectured on Virgil at Trinity; at Shrewsbury, where he had taught for a short time, a very little erudition went a long way. Besides, most of the passengers knew considerably less Latin and Greek than the Middle Forms at Shrewsbury; so he would talk to them about the Greeks at sea. What, for example, did it feel like to travel on a Greek ship between Massilia and Byzantium, as they were now travelling between Marseilles and Constantinople? That was a question he could not answer; it was just as difficult to imagine a day spent on the moon. He could only tell them certain dull facts—that according to Herodotus a ship could cover about seventy miles by day and sixty by night; that the oars were used to put on speed; and that St. Paul did the two hundred miles between the Straits of Messina and Puteoli inside two days. And when it came to the atmospherics of classical sailing, he had no doubt that the Greeks were reluctant seafarers—as reluctant as he was himself, for this was the first time that he had spent more than twelve consecutive hours on a ship. Even Thucydides, though you felt a sea breeze blowing through every page of his history, was by preference a landlubber: and he must, anyway, have had bitter memories of that disastrous expedition. Homer was not interested in the details of navigation: "So on we sailed, sad at heart, glad to escape death, but lacking our dear companions"—that was no way to keep a log. Aeneas put these things more precisely. Nor had the Greeks wasted their eloquence on the sea—Aeschylus' "the myriad laughter of the sea's waves" was exceptional—and it was not until you reached Theocritus that the Greeks actually seemed to be enjoying the seaside. Still, it was interesting to revisit all these places, even though you were asleep when you sailed past the coast on which Hector had cast fire among the Grecian ships.

Ronald Knox concluded this charming essay by recalling the voice that suddenly was heard from Paxae, calling out that the great god Pan was dead. It was true—truer indeed than most of the legends of antiquity. A world was dead, and never could be recaptured, even by one who had the classical authors at his finger tips. "I knew that," said Ronald Knox, "when I saw the Hellespont. It did not remind me of the ship Argo, nor of the agony of Troy, nor of Xerxes' bridge, nor of the Spartan victory at Aegospotami. The last, to me, is as legendary as the first. It was peopled for me instead by those who fought and died there fifteen years ago, men of my own country and of my own speech." If one has small Latin and no Greek whatever, one is sometimes conscious in talking to men who have an abundance of both that one really has no right to be discussing literature at all. Intellectually speaking, one is a *parvenu:* and one questions the validity of one's own standards. It is comforting, therefore, to know that the gulf opened up by the Incarnation was so wide, and literally so catastrophic, that even Ronald Knox felt a stranger on ground where none had a better right than he to feel at home.

Apart from Bremond and the religious historians, or spiritual writers, Knox had only an average acquaintance with French literature. You do not easily imagine Balzac or Baudelaire at his bedside. But so forceful an apologist could hardly have avoided Pascal. Pascal was characteristically French in not being able to "pass through the crisis of his soul without wanting to get it down, at the first possible moment, on paper." But what was interesting in the case of Pascal was the reappearance of a John Wesley as a Jonathan Swift. In the *Provincial Letters*, for all their dialectical brilliance, he had not really disposed of the Jesuits; he had only forged a weapon for M. de Voltaire. But in the *Pensées* he was trying to solve "at a blow the age-long difficulty of apologetics, where he set out to convince man's mind and man's heart at a single stroke, instead of appealing first to the one, and then to the other." Would the finished work have been a rival to the *Summa Contra Gentes*, or a rival to the *Exercises?* Or would it, miraculously, have been a rival to both? We should never know; all that Pascal had left were "the ruins"—might not Ronald Knox have allowed them to be foundation stones?— "of a temple which was never built." But before he died Knox started gathering them together, and a few others of his own fashioning, and began to sketch, if not a temple, then at least an oratory of apologetic. That, however, was not the kind of thing he generally talked about when he sat on the fender and you sat in his favourite armchair; and a discussion of it must be left to a subsequent chapter.

6

THE HISTORIAN

FOR A LONG TIME it was rumoured that Ronald Knox was
writing a record, and a refutation, of all the heresies. It was to
be his *magnum opus;* his longest, most laboured, and most
lasting book. In so far as he cared about fame—and he did
care about it a little—this book would attest it. If he were
observed prowling about private or public libraries, this was
his secret business. Authors hate being asked what they are
working at, particularly when they have been working at it
for years; and even Knox's closest friends were not inquisi-
tive. They waited as patiently as he did. The title of the book,
when it was published in 1950, told them that it was not quite
the book they had expected to read, and the Dedicatory Preface to Evelyn Waugh told them it was not quite the book
that Knox had expected to write. Ronald Knox was the least
enthusiastic of men, and when he calls a book *Enthusiasm*[1]
you imagine that enthusiasm will probably have rather a raw
deal. And indeed a raw deal was all part of the original
plan:

[1] New York: Oxford, 1950.

"All this confusion, this priggishness, this pedantry, this eccentricity and worse, follows directly from the rash step that takes you outside the fold of Peter. All my historical figures, Wesley himself included, were to be a kind of rogues gallery, an awful warning against illuminism."

But that was not how the book worked out. Knox found himself in the position of a novelist who conceives a character of whom he disapproves and sets out to illustrate his dislike. The character, however, is too strong for him; being human, he has his good side as well as his bad; and his humanity matters more than his merits or his misdeeds. It would hardly be unfair to describe the conception of *Enthusiasm* as the conception of a convert who has adhered to a principle, and its execution as the work of an apostle who has acquired an experience. "The more you got to know the men," Knox tells us, "the more human did they become, for better or worse; you were more concerned to find out why they thought as they did than to prove it was wrong." Thus five out of the first six chapters were entirely rewritten, so instinctively had the author's sympathies quarrelled with his judgments of ten or fifteen years back.

Had Ronald Knox been allowed, or encouraged, to devote his whole time to writing and research, *Enthusiasm* might have been the masterpiece that its author modestly hoped for. But the literary *abbé* falls into no classification recognized by the Hierarchy of England and Wales. Had Knox belonged to one of the Religious Orders, he might well have been put under obedience to give all the necessary time to the book which was undoubtedly closer to his heart than any other that he wrote. It may be argued that he did, in fact, have a good deal more time than most priests who are not exempt from pastoral cares. But he did not have time enough. *Enthusiasm* is his biggest book, but it is a long way from being his best.

It was a work of collation, not of original research. For his treatment of the Jansenists he must depend on Bremond and Abercrombie; and on Bremond again for his account of the Quietists, of Petrucci and Malaval, of Molinos and Madame Guyon. A passing mention of Bremond's "eleven volumes" indicates both the scope and the limits of his summary. A book of this kind cannot escape a suggestion of the midnight oil, although Ronald Knox rarely retired to bed after eleven. But compare *Enthusiasm* with Newman's *History of the Arians* and you see the advantages of being a don. Compare it with Bremond and you see the advantages of a comfortable apartment in the shadow of Notre Dame. As I have already said, *Enthusiasm* is a work of *haute vulgarisation*, a unique summary of individualist spirituality from the earliest Christian times, remarkable for its psychological insight. But there are pages in it, here and there, that someone else might just conceivably have written.

To estimate the justice of Knox's analysis of so many men and movements—whether or not Bossuet was "an odious fellow," about whom the worst you could say was that you had met him—would overstep the boundaries of this essay; but it is interesting to see how far an historical enquiry allowed play for his literary method. As a preacher, he knew the value of comparison. "If Maximilla was the Madame Guyon of Montanism, Lucilla no less surely played Countess of Huntingdon to the Donatists." Thus the various strands of a single theme are all woven into a persuasive pattern. Nationalism had its part in the Donatist controversy, but here, as in so many controversies, nationalism was an undercurrent; you could not accurately chart its flow. "Who shall say whether the Scots disliked the Book of Common Prayer because it was Episcopalian, or because it was English?" And—to pursue a Scottish analogy—"the attitude of the ordinary respectable Donatist towards his brethren of the right wing will probably have been much the same as the attitude of the ordinary respectable Presbyterian towards the Protestant mob-leaders who emerge, from time to time, in the slums of Edinburgh and Glasgow." Luther, when he came out of the Wartburg, found himself in the same dilemma as Kerensky: should he use and attempt to control his more extreme supporters, at the risk of being overthrown by them, or should he denounce them as dangerous visionaries and carry on the fight without them? The story of Fox and Nayler was like the story of Newman and Faber—the old story of London *versus* the provinces. If Newman had foreseen the independence of the London Oratory, would he have let Faber go? There is a happy comparison between Molinos telling you that he approved of meditation and Paderewski telling you that he approved of five-finger exercises—with the clear implication that both exercises existed only to be outgrown; and Madame Guyon is charmingly described as a "phantom Helen," animating, from her prison at Vincennes, the combats of Bossuet and Fénelon. Knox, for all his sympathy with the misfortunes of Port Royal, was quick to observe a kind of patriarchal smugness about the place—not unlike the atmosphere of Evangelical Society in England a hundred years ago.

When servants break things, Euphemia points out to her married sister, Madame Périer, you should first of all tell them that you do not mind what they break, as long as they do not break the commandments; and then, that it is a pity there are so few employers like that; and then, that we should feel far happier in their condition of life than in ours. It is all, no doubt, admirable Catholic doctrine; but you have caught, for a moment, the remembered atmosphere of *The Fairchild Family*.

Knox did not, of course, identify Protestantism and enthusiasm; Luther's Protestantism, for the purposes of the enthusiast, was stillborn. He is particularly good on Wesley; indeed I doubt if there is a better commendation of Wesley for the modern reader. Knox saw him at the parting of the ways; between William Law urging him to treat his phobias as scruples and go on courageously in the dark, and his Moravian friends urging him to resolve them in the spiritual crisis of what they called "conversion"; perched, in fact, "on the razor's edge between the watershed of Quietism and the watershed of Jansenism." Was this to interpret him too tendentiously in Catholic terms? Yet Knox had spotted a passage, missed or omitted by Wesley's biographers, which showed that he had thought of becoming a Catholic, and had only been deflected by St. Cyprian. Knox meant what he said, and no more. He meant that the Church had once existed as a mirage—he might almost have added, as a menace—on Wesley's mental horizon. He compared Wesley's fear of mysticism with Bossuet's—a fear, not uncommon among ecclesiastics, that you never quite knew where you were with these people. Wesley "had the mind of a Jesuit, with the morals of a Jansenist"; a lonely man, never caring for the society of Whitefield, as Newman had craved for the society of Keble and Church.

Jean Cocteau once remarked to me: "Il y a des acteurs qui

pensent ce qu'ils disent, et des acteurs qui pensent à ce qu'ils disent." Similarly, as Knox summarised it, the Quietist did not think about God: he thought God. It seems as good a definition of pure contemplation as one is likely to get, and Knox never lost sight of the purity of impulse that lay behind the distortions and eccentricities of enthusiasm. His book is among the most charitable that has ever been written on a subject which is constantly forcing one to take sides. What stuck in his gullet about the Jansenists was the readiness with which they assumed their neighbour's damnation. To Saint-Cyran teaching his *petites écoles* that Virgil would go to hell because he wrote poems to the greater glory of Augustus instead of to the greater glory of God, Knox opposed the legend of St. Paul reaching Naples and weeping over Virgil's tomb:

> Quem te (inquit) reddidissem,
> Si te vivum invenissem,
> Poetarum maxime.

And these implacable perfectionists had a further unforgivable fault; they could only rescue the world from collective damnation by making war on the Jesuits. Campion Hall at Oxford is only a stone's throw from the Old Palace, and there was no need of a subterranean passage to connect them. Nothing could have been more open and advertised than Ronald Knox's affection for the Jesuits; and nobody else has done what he did in *Enthusiasm*, although it may have fallen a few inches short of the book he had wished to write, and that others hoped he might have written.

In dedicating *Let Dons Delight* (1939) to Lady Acton, Ronald Knox described—or rather deprecated—the book as "all this waste of time." It was, in fact, his last literary fling before he got down to the grind of translating the Bible; and it was probably the best book he ever wrote. It defies classification. First you think it is going to be a skit, and then you think it is going to be a satire; and although it gambols as friskily as the one and cuts as sharply as the other, it turns out to be a perfectly serious (and, incidentally, vastly amusing) work of historical imagination. That is why I have chosen to discuss it immediately after *Enthusiasm*. Where the weapon of satire is exaggeration, the virtue of history is exactitude. This is the way dons talk; this is the way they have always talked; these are the subjects they discuss; these are the kind of men they are. The book is intimately and inimitably Oxonian. It could only have been written by one who had loved Oxford, and left it, returned to it, and then left it once more. It distils Oxford, as *Zuleika Dobson*—and few other books—distil it. It is at once affectionate and disenchanted.

Knox imagines himself going to dine at Simon Magus College on a Sunday evening, and as the dons gather round their port in the customary semi-circle, he falls asleep. In the bare ten minutes during which his host deserts him to answer a telephone call, he dreams himself back into the same Common Room at successive intervals of fifty years—from the eve of the Armada in 1588 and the imminence of the Civil War in 1638, to the early years of the Tractarian Movement and the rear-guard action of the eighties. Then he wakes up—and we hear what the dons are saying in 1938, while somebody or other is tub-thumping about Spain in the Town Hall. It is a conspectus of English history as Oxford has seen and felt it, across which there falls the play of contrasting personalities, mostly small, and of parochial ambitions, invariably petty. At the end of each chapter, when the dons have finished their discussion, and have disagreed to differ, Knox appends a

variety of biographical data which he puts into the mouths
and the precise idiom of real contemporaries who might have
known them. Mark Pattison, in as cruel a parody as Ronald
Knox ever perpetrated, uncovers the Machiavellian intrigues
which deprived him of a Fellowship at Simon Magus. Johnson
and Boswell, as they return to London in the coach, discuss
the dons with whom they have just been dining, or might
have dined not so long ago. What does Johnson think of Dr.
Thewes, now dead these many years?

Thewes was a good man, but a heavy man; he could not endure
that anybody should differ with his opinion, yet he wanted the
capacity to jostle them down in an argument. There is nothing so
frets a man's mind, as to be continually disagreeing with his neighbour, yet never able to get the better of him. I hear he was at one
time engaged upon an answer to Hume, but it came to nothing. If
he *were* alive now, he would be for answering Gibbon.

Boswell: There are many of us, Sir, who are sorry you have
written nothing against Hume.

Johnson: Sir, that is to save yourself the trouble of *thinking*
against Hume. There is no sooner a good answer put out to
some book that shocks the conscience of humanity, than the
world takes a holiday from reading either the one or the other.
But I would have put out a better answer than Dr. Thewes,
depend upon it. Thewes would have given him the point, debating with him in the manner of the schools; I would have knocked
him down with common-sense (*pausing a little*). Thewes would
have liked to bring the Stuarts back.

Boswell: That was great loyalty in him.

Johnson: No, Sir, only a habituation of the mind.

The reader rubs his eyes; can this really have been made up? Or this, on Mr. Shillett, who was wondering in 1738 who was to have the Professorship of Poetry—a wonder that never ceases:

Boswell: He was a man that promised much in his youth; I was told in Oxford that *he might have done anything*.
Johnson: Sir, he might have hanged himself.

Somehow the last person you expected to meet with Ronald Knox was Harold Nicolson. But it is extraordinary how Balliol men hang together, and Knox had evidently read and enjoyed *Some People*. So here is Sir Harold remembering his first and last meetings with a don called Leadbetter— obviously so named because he could easily become Ledders.

"He must, I conjectured, be the guest of Lamplough" —another name that immediately conjures up the laburnum bushes in the Banbury Road—"who sat, next to him; Lamp- lough was all right—I had met him in Sligger's rooms, and we smiled at one another with that insecure presumption of intimacy one reserved for people one had met in Sligger's rooms." Sligger, in case you had forgot—for old men forget and young men have not had time to remember—was F. F. Urquhart, a Fellow and History Tutor of Balliol, and an in- timate friend of Ronald Knox. People talked of "Sligger's young men" as they talked of "Milner's young men." No other Englishmen of the century, so far as I am aware, have had young men attached to their names in quite the same way. Sir Harold's last meeting with Leadbetter, appropriately enough, was "in Paris, at the Gare du Nord, when I was over there for the Peace Conference." He was engaged in repatriating the Armenians.

The central theme of *Let Dons Delight* is the gradual extrusion of theology from the academic mind. The dons of 1588 were passionately perplexed about the authority of the Pope, with the Duke of Medina Sidonia in the boots of General Franco, if that successful opportunist had seen eye to eye with Hitler at Irun. The dons of 1638 were discussing the rights of the Anglican episcopate, and those of 1688 the authority of the King. Theology was already beating its retreat. And although it stages a powerful counter-attack under the Tractarians, Mr. Savile, who will presently follow Newman to other places, sees how deeply, how inevitably, Oxford will disengage itself from the Oxford Movement:

This ferment that is now working among us does not belong to the spirit of the University; we are changelings, it seems to me, in the cradle. The genius which broods over this place is one which bids us reflect, and criticize, and do nothing. To have resolved your mind clearly upon a matter of speculative truth, is to disqualify yourself for its citizenship. If I am still fellow of Simon Magus, it is not because I hope to conquer the hesitations of my colleagues; it is because I cannot conquer my own. In the days when I see clearly, as you would have me see clearly, the scenes that I have loved will be my walks no longer.

By 1938 it was difficult—and embarrassing—to introduce the mere notion of God into a Common Room conversation. Whereas in 1838—when the threat to carry the railway from Didcot was as serious as the threat to carry the road through the Christ Church Meadows in 1960—Dr. Haynes had seen by the papers that the Prince of Talleyrand had died; and Mr.

Telford remarked that he had made a Christian end of it after all. No one would have made the same observation, even supposing it had been true, about Signor Mussolini. Politics had opposed their implacable absolutes to metaphysical enquiry—and even scientific research was subject to them. The classics were being frowned upon as a seed-bed of class distinctions, and it was already a very long time since anyone had dared to quote Horace in the House of Commons.

For a man like Ronald Knox, whose memories went back to Asquith, it must have seemed that an Oxford that would no longer betake itself to the dictionary would very quickly betake itself to the devil. But the Oxford evoked so unforgettably in these pages is neither an outpost of progress nor a citadel of reaction. It is the hub of a circle described by recurring idiosyncrasies. Young dons become elderly Provosts; others leave the fireside and the circulating port, either because they are too ambitious for the things that do not belong to Oxford, or not ambitious enough for the things that do belong to it; others again hint of their private line to the world of great affairs; most things are called into question, and many things remain unchanged. *Plus ça change, plus c'est la même chose.* The undergraduates who read the first editions of *The Waste Land* and *Ulysses* were in direct academic descent from the undergraduates whom Mr. Savile had caught reading Shelley and Byron. And just as the Provost had ventured on a cautious defence of Byron because he had written well of Sennacherib—"he came down like a wolf on the fold, I think; that was a very powerful simile"—so his successor might have defended Mr. Eliot because he had written rather pathetically of Phlebas, and James Joyce because, for all his monkish Latin, he showed traces of a classical education. Nevertheless, for better or worse—but more, it must be confessed, for worse—the Oxford of 1938 was the Oxford that Ronald Knox left for the second time, when his work at the Catholic Chaplaincy was at an end. These were the conversations he overheard—or conversations not very unlike them—when he escaped from his flock on a Sunday evening to dine in Trinity or elsewhere. It was his native milieu in a way that no other milieu in which he moved was native to him. Henceforward, when he returned to it—and he would return to it often—it was as a *revenant* from better, or at any rate from more congenial, times. He had loved Oxford, as few men of his time had known and loved it; and in *Let Dons Delight* he had written it down.

7

APOLOGIA
AND CONTROVERSY

THE TWO ARE INSEPARABLE; you cannot, in the Babel of the modern world, defend your own opinion without openly or implicitly attacking someone else's. Ronald Knox's apologia for the truths of the Catholic religion began some years before he discovered its fullness; and *Some Loose Stones* (1913) was, as its title suggests, an answer to *Foundations*. *Foundations* had been the classical statement of Anglican Liberal theology, and Ronald Knox, when he wrote his reply to it, had no need to be looking over his shoulder at *Pascendi*. Not that so powerful and, in some ways, reactionary a document would have held many terrors for him. He was afraid neither of political, nor of theological reaction. In asking, in his opening chapter, the famous question: "How much will Jones swallow?" he drove right to the heart of Modernism. The political progressive had his theological counterpart. Because the Fabian had a hatred of waste, he would be struck by the wastefulness of creation rather than by its grandeur. Because he disliked the principle of monarchy, he would be shocked by the idea of Divine Omnipotence. If God existed at all, he could only be a strictly constitutional deity. Because the political progressive was squeamish about punishment, he would naturally be sceptical about Hell; and because he believed in the wisdom of transient majorities, he would not admit that some decisions were infallible and therefore could not be revoked. The first need of the modern mind was to train its imagination, because it was the imagination rather than the intellect of the modern world that was at war with Christian truth.

Ronald Knox had too many detective stories up his sleeve not to distrust the value of hypothesis as a guide to truth. You could explain all the miracles worked by Our Lord on the hypothesis that He was Omnipotent God; but you could equally well explain the healing of the sick by faith healing, the stilling of the storm by coincidence, the feeding of the Five Thousand as a misrepresented Sacrament, the withering of the fig tree as a misrepresented parable, and the raising of Lazarus as a case of premature burial. In the same way a man might be found murdered in a criminal district of London, with the window open and the plate gone from the cupboard; and a plausible case could be made out for robbery with violence. But the man might equally well have been murdered for some quite different motive, the window have been left open, and a casual passer-by have gone in and robbed the room. It was because the hypothesis was so constant a provocation to error that Knox rejected it as a loose stone rather than a firm foundation. "If," he concluded, "I could not preach the Christian faith in its fullness on a basis of absolute *a priori* certainty, I would give up preaching it altogether."

Behind *Foundations* there was *Lux Mundi,* and it was

Bishop Gore in his Bampton Lectures who had applied *a posteriori* methods of reasoning to the mystery of the Incarnation. Knox found Sherlock Holmes, not to mention the medieval theologians, a safer guide. "I ought to know by this time," Holmes had observed in *A Study in Scarlet*, "that when a fact appears to be opposed to a long train of deductions, it invariably proves to be capable of bearing some other interpretation." Thus any text that seemed to imply a limitation of power or outlook, or defect of character, in the Son of God must be explained in such a way as did not contradict His perfection and omnipotence. The Holmes quotation appears discreetly in a footnote, because here Knox is arguing with dons before a public that believed in dons, at a time when the reading of detective fiction had not yet become the sole recreation of accredited intellectuals. But as popular journalism invaded the field of religious speculation, Knox would show less concern for academic decorum. First, however, he must be quite certain of the ground he was standing on. The authors of *Foundations* were his friends at the High Tables of Trinity and Balliol, Oriel and Magdalen: and they cannot have been very much surprised to find him no longer at their side. But they may have been slightly irritated to be told that they were no longer in the vanguard of modern thought, and that in the city of lost causes theirs was the last cause to be lost.

Ronald Knox's account of his religious upbringing, development, and conversion—*A Spiritual Aeneid* (1916)—is material for the biographer rather than the literary critic. Mr. Evelyn Waugh has made ample and skillful use of it. If we want to see Ronald Knox in his writings as distinct from Ronald Knox the writer, we shall catch him here more directly—or at least more continuously—than elsewhere. The book asks to be judged beside others in the same genre— notably beside Newman's *Apologia*, because Knox and Newman were taking the same journey and facing identical difficulties. It was the hard cross-country journey from the Via Media to the Appian Way. Each man had gloried in the leadership of a party, although Knox was an Anglican Papalist in a sense that Newman had never been. "There is no such bully," he writes, "as a logical mind"; and the mind, in his case, was not only logical but "contrary." He no sooner caught sight of an argument than he wanted to knock it down —even when the argument was his own. This lengthened the process of conversion; and it was only when he was tired out with trying to fit the key into the back door that he realized the front door had been open all the time. The depth of his convictions and the sincerity of his search were never in doubt for an instant, but for all that the book did a slight disservice to its author. It is, in the experience of many readers, the only writing of Ronald Knox about which you feel, when you put it down, that you are not quite sure whether you like him. He was too clever by half to recognize immediately the truth that was staring him in the face. It was not until he was down, and very nearly out, that the maze of contradictory speculation suddenly straightened out into the comfortable breadth and unambiguous direction of the Roman road.

A Spiritual Aeneid is a reticent book, mercifully free from either pietism or self-pity, but it betrays the signature of an exceptionally sensitive man. So, of course, does the *Apologia*. But whereas Newman wears his sensibility on his sleeve, Knox wears his deep in the lining of his overcoat. Newman expects what is generally understood by "religious experience" and is not inclined to mistrust it. Knox does not expect it, and he does not trust it very far when it comes his way. The only emotion he allows us to share is the emotion aroused by certain scenes and places. Always attached to Shrewsbury, where he had taught for a short time during the early years of the 1914 war, he can remember "sitting in the deep window-sill" of his room and watching "the tree-fringed river," with its "adorable curve," and "the pencilled snows on Caradoc, autumn mists and bright firesides, boys melancholy as only boys can be, and cheerful as only boys have a right to be." From Eton he carried away memories of "tea in Sixth Form Passage on November afternoons, with your pores tingling from a hot bath; sunny days when you sat on the low wall in front of chapel, or wandered out to watch cricket from the pavilion; unintellectual acquaintances, vague satisfaction in boyish authority, a few treasured friendships, antiquity in the very air you breathed, yet youth all round you and within you, and the river flowing through it all to remind you of transience and eternity." As he leaves London for the decisive retreat at Farnborough, he sees "in panorama the twin towers of the Abbey nestling under the Houses of Parliament, and the solitary campanile of the Cathedral." Here we are reminded of other towers seen from other windows, as Newman said farewell to Oxford, and of the two kingdoms which eternally confront each other under the single name of Westminster. The flamboyant *parvenu* Gothic of the Chapel at Farnborough, where Napoleon III and the Prince Imperial lie buried, is like a last trivial flourish of the Second Empire, and *sic transit gloria mundi* was its easily legible motto. It was the very place "for meeting your spiritual Sedan."

The Virgilian scholar, or the mere lover of Virgil with no
pretension to scholarship, will delight to trace the Aeneid of
Ronald Knox in the quotations which describe, with extraordinary aptness, the various stages of his journey. On the eve
of his reception into the Church he sent the following line
from the Sixth Book to Father Martindale:

Jam tandem Italiae fugientis prendimus vias

Even at Farnborough the *Aeneid* had kept him company, and
he finished reading it the night before he was received. The
city at whose gates he was knocking was not exactly the city
that Aeneas had founded, but it was built in the same place
and was the capital of a wider empire; and the Father of the
West had pointed him along the road that led to it as he stood,
like Dante, "in the middle of his way." It was open to any
critic of Ronald Knox to discount his conversion as a symp-
tom of that readiness to defend the indefensible with which he
was sometimes credited; but if we are to look for suasions
beyond the logic of a sharply logical mind, we shall find it in a
certain chivalry which stood up against the English worship
of the "*fait accompli.*" He had always, he tells us, "taken a
Catonic pleasure in the defeated cause, and set my head
against the stream." He was with Cicero against his accusers,
and with Charles I on the scaffold, and with the last of the
Lancastrian kings, sorrowful and sainted, who was the
Founder of Eton. It was natural, with these antecedent prejudices, that Ronald Knox's sympathies should have been on the
losing side at Tyburn.

The Belief of Catholics was written in 1927, just after
Knox had gone to the Oxford Chaplaincy. He was fortified

by seven years teaching at St. Edmund's, Ware—a seminary
in which he had theologians for company and embryo priests
for pupils. At Oxford he came back into the world, and met
the challenge of the world's incredulity. The book was one of
a series, and Ronald Knox had little space in which to say a
great deal. It may be argued that he did not say enough.
Certain difficulties—Grace and Free-Will, Providence and the
existence of Evil, the Divine Mercy and the doctrine of Eternal Punishment—are hardly, or inadequately, touched upon.
And the earlier chapters in which he lays the groundwork for
belief are more stimulating than the later chapters where he
explains the articles of belief itself.

His starting point is the modern distaste for religion,
though he nowhere meets the objection that for many people
religion is mortally boring. Nothing in the armoury of mate-
rialism is more difficult to pierce than this. Knox will not have
it that the religious sense is like an ear for music—either you
possess it or you don't. He could imagine indifference and
hostility, because he had met them; where men were prepared
to reason, he would argue patiently. But there was a miasma
of sheer spiritual insensibility seeping up around him which
no argument and no exhortation could dispel. That he felt its
pressure, as he took the measure of his Oxford task, there can
be no doubt. Although he is naturally not writing for the
converted, he is at least writing for the interested—but what
of those who are not interested in the least, to whom the mere
terminology of religious discussion means nothing at all?
These will hardly be touched when he asks whether "a
diocesan Bishop would have dared, in the middle of the nineteenth century, to express in a newspaper article his disbelief
in eternal punishment," or whether "the rector of a much

frequented London church would have preached, and afterwards published, a sermon in which he recommended the remarriage of divorced persons." Colenso, in the brash new world of Lady Metroland, was hardly any more a name to conjure with. It was the same with artificial birth control. This was a burning topic in the 'twenties, suddenly risen into semi-respectability from the *demi-monde*. It could not be brushed aside in a reference to the laws of natural morality which were evident to all "right-minded persons."The trouble was that more and more of the right-minded persons were coming to hold the wrong views.

Granted a preliminary disposition to enquire into the credentials of the Catholic Church, *The Belief of Catholics* will carry a good measure of conviction, although the nature of religious assent is rather summarily treated. For that, the reader must go to Father D'Arcy. The Thomistic proofs of the existence of God are lucidly marshalled, though I fancy that in later years Ronald Knox would have allowed more weight to the "numinous" sense. The nature of the early Church; the development of Our Lord's claim to Divinity; the synoptic testimony to the Resurrection and its worth, so to speak, in a court of Law—all this is admirably surveyed. But the specific objections to Catholicism, none the less insurmountable, in many cases, because they are tied to particular points; the charge of superstition and Mariolatry and, above all, the charge of intolerance—none of these receives a conclusive answer.

It is obvious that many ill-instructed Catholics, all the world over, worship Our Lady in much the same sense as they worship Our Lord; and it is the height of disingenuousness to pretend otherwise. Of course they are not officially encouraged to do so. But we may not be misinterpreting the mind of the Church if we imagine it as thinking that it is better to honour Our Lady excessively than not to honour her at all. Similarly, superstition is forbidden; yet in thirty years as a Catholic I have never heard it preached against. Are we to suppose that Catholics are so little superstitious that they never scandalise the enquirer who, in these respects, is more scrupulous for the purity of religion than they are? In controversy, as in war, the tactics of *reculer pour mieux sauter* will sometimes win a victory; and I do not think that Ronald Knox realised how much ground can be reclaimed by legitimate admissions. Surely it was unwise, to say the very least, to declare that "when we demand liberty in the modern State, we are appealing to its own principles, not to ours." People were quick to turn these words against Ronald Knox: where then did the Catholic Church fix the boundaries of a reasonable liberty? The non-Catholic had the right to a reply, and he was not given it. Ronald Knox had been very successful in suggesting the ambience of Catholicism; and one memorable phrase—"the water of conviction is turned into the wine of faith"—earned a page to itself in Maurice Baring's *"Have You Anything to Declare?"* But he was, in general, cleverer in getting under the skin of the ancient heretic than of the modern infidel, or Protestant. He knew the ancient paganism by heart; he only knew the modern by hearsay, and he did not like what he heard. So he had left a good many questions knocking at the door, and there was at least one acute and insatiable controversialist only too eager to knock it down.

Controversy is a subdivision of apologetics. In *The Belief of Catholics*, Ronald Knox had been explaining his religion to the world at large; he had enjoyed an unchallenged initiative.

In *Difficulties* he was defending it against the attacks of a single individual, in a dialogue where his opponent had choice of weapons and where any weakness in the presentation of his case would be open to attack. The idea of the book was suggested to him by Arnold Lunn in 1930. Lunn had been at Balliol with Ronald Knox, and beside this common maternity a competitive pre-existence at Eton and Harrow was of no account. They were contemporaries—Lunn succeeding Knox as editor of the *Isis*—but not, as yet, close friends. When you recall that Arnold Lunn's favourite spot in all England was Oxford, you suggest a certain community of taste; when you recall that his next favourite spot in all England was the Continental departure platform at Victoria Station, you indicate a certain difference of temperament. Lunn had included Knox, not too respectfully, among his *Roman Converts* (1925), and Knox had only with difficulty refrained from a personal reply very much sharper than the one he actually committed to paper. Then, in 1930, Lunn had reviewed *Caliban in Grub Street* with such pleasure that he could not resist the opportunity of provoking more important matter from the same pen. His own *Flight from Reason* had recently been published, a work so eminently rational that the Rationalist Press assumed that the author must be a Roman Catholic. Indeed none of the difficulties adduced by Arnold Lunn in his exchange of letters with Ronald Knox is so nearly insuperable as the difficulty of believing that he himself ever disbelieved in Catholicism. In that respect, as in some others, the book has a certain period charm.

Lunn had lost his faith in Christianity at an early age through reading Leslie Stephen's *Agnostic's Apology;* and he must have derived a certain consolation, both before and after he recovered it, from the thought that the accident was due to a fellow-mountaineer. By 1930 he was a convinced theist, and even able to admit the case for Catholicism on *a priori* grounds; but he was troubled by the contrast, both current and historical, between the pretensions and the practice of Catholicism as well as by certain aspects of its teaching. These were the "difficulties" he discussed with Ronald Knox. It is almost a truism to say that only the Catholic really knows the case against Catholicism, but he is handicapped by also knowing the answer to it. Arnold Lunn could certainly have mounted a more formidable attack from inside the ramparts, but in that case he would never have waited for Ronald Knox to reply for the angels. Still, in the dialogue as we have it, he did voice a number of objections common to many who are sickening for conversion, and voiced them with characteristic skill. But he so evidently admires the thing he is attacking that the reader cannot help being left with an impression of shadow-boxing. Here are two Balliol men speaking from opposite sides at the Union; here are two trained minds, each understanding the other's point of view. Indeed, the interest of the book is less in the things they disagree about than in the things they hold in common. When in the Preface to the First Edition Lunn quotes Knox as writing in reference to a Symposium of Essays for and against the Church, to which he had contributed ". . . but as we were not allowed to see each other's essays, I presume that we shall all miss each other's onslaughts, like the two armies at Mantinea," the implication is clear that we are all supposed to know what happened at Mantinea. Sir Arnold has told me that he always reads a passage from the classics before shaving, and the full flavour of the book will only be grasped by those who know enough Latin to realise that it is dedicated to Balliol.

Nevertheless, the difficulties of Arnold Lunn were real difficulties although they may not have been very original ones. I think the reader will conclude with a verdict of "Honours even." Ronald Knox's answers are convincing from within the context of a belief which is strong enough to support an apparent contradiction. He *knows* that God is omniscient, and he *knows* that he, Knox, has free will. The resulting paradox merely defines a mystery which he is careful to distinguish from a "vagueness." When the second edition of the book was issued in 1950, sixteen years after Lunn's reception into the Church, both contestants looked back at the controversy, and their reflections were published as an epilogue. The temper of the times had changed. There was a much freer climate of discussion within the Church. You could hold theories about biblical inspiration which would have been hardly tolerated twenty years earlier. The Church might not change her mind, but she had shown that she could change her mood. She was still happier if you swallowed Jonah—and Jonah had never been a *plat de choix* for Arnold Lunn—but she would not push him quite so rudely down your throat. Here Ronald Knox's contention that Our Lord could not have referred to Jonah as He might have referred to a story in Homer does not seem to me convincingly argued. And on the question of eternal punishment—Lunn's principal stumbling-block—he came very late to the admission that we do not know exactly when the soul leaves the body, and that we may therefore reasonably imagine some elbow-room for the mercy of God. Nor did he ever use the argument that since, human nature being what it is, many people would never get to Heaven unless they were afraid of Hell, the existence of Hell is an instrument of Divine Mercy—whether it is heavily populated, as many of the Saints have supposed, or whether—as

Manning preferred to think—it is eternally uninhabited. Here, too, the climate of Catholic teaching had changed; and the C.T.S. pamphlet which had so shocked Arnold Lunn when he began his correspondence with Ronald Knox had been withdrawn from circulation. I am surprised, however, that Lunn did not push home his attack a little harder. He could plausibly have maintained that it is the doctrine of eternal punishment which really holds the Catholic Church together; that it is the active fear of Hell rather than the vaguer hope of Heaven which recalls the sinner on his death-bed; and this might have led him to question the whole validity of a religion which had become, for the majority of its adherents, so largely a matter of rewards and punishments, so little an adventure and a love-affair. Ronald Knox, no doubt, would have had his answer; although in his generally sensible defence of the doctrine of Indulgences he strangely fails to link this with the doctrine of the Communion of Saints. If the Saints can help us with their prayers, it is natural to suppose that they can aid us with their assets. One further small point may be questioned. On what evidence does Knox base his assertion that in 1930 torture was employed in the United States?

No, the reader who wants to see Christianity defended from serious attack will do better to read Arnold Lunn when he is defending it against C. E. M. Joad or J. B. S. Haldane than Ronald Knox when he is defending it against Arnold Lunn—not so much because the defence is more skillful as because the attack is more sustained. Nevertheless, *Difficulties* —not least because it is a controversy conducted by two men grounded in the classics with a common belief in reason—still makes lively and attractive reading. On the side of Ronald

Knox, who principally concerns us here, it is full of perceptive and occasionally surprising things. How much easier to
admire Manning if we see him as a man who never quite lost
"the mentality of an archdeacon"! How piquant that Knox
should have found the Canticle of Canticles an edifying love-
song, and that Lunn should have been slightly shocked by it!
How many controversialists would have had the scholarship
to compare our Lord's "inability" to perform certain miracles
with Themistocles' not being able "to bring himself" to live in
his former style? How apt, as ever, are the metaphors—
where, for example, the glory given to God by men or angels
is compared to a searchlight turned on the sun! And how
pertinent is the rare excursion into prophecy—"I do not think
it is impossible we shall see some kind of religious revival in
our time of the Wesleyan type. The loss of our world position may lead to it. But I do not think there will be any
background of orthodoxy behind it, and for that reason I
think that if it comes, it will be short-lived." One seems to
overhear, already, the sincere but synthetic exhortations of
Dr. Graham echoing round the Harringay Arena.

Looking back on the correspondence, Ronald Knox was
impressed by his own prediction that before long the arguments of both would look old-fashioned. "I think," he added,
"I have less stomach now for controversy, and I am surprised
at the energy with which I kept up the shuttle-cock in those
days. Strange, that I should have been responsible for letting
loose on the Church such an apologist as you! I feel like an
elderly cyclotron that has played the midwife to an energy
not its own." That energy had not abated, but both men were
at a disadvantage in addressing a generation "so Modern-
Greats-minded that nothing which happened before the In-

dustrial Revolution can be mentioned without a slight savour of indecency. But, what is much more important, they no longer take it for granted (as you and I did) that England is top nation. They no longer find a key to history in the idea of freedom slowly broadening out from the Norman Conquest to the relief of Ladysmith." A close friend of Ronald Knox remarked to me in, I think, 1944: "Ronnie can't quite forgive this war for not being the last one." What she meant was that the Kaiser's war was a war that he understood, though it had cost him so dear in casualties. The "difficulties" of 1950 were not the "difficulties" of 1930, and new controversialists would be required to meet a new challenge. But, as we shall presently see, when the first atom bomb was dropped on Hiroshima and the securities in which Ronald Knox had been cradled were shattered once and for all, it was he who got down on his hands and knees to rescue the pearl beyond price from the rubble.

Ronald Knox was in the habit of spending his summer holidays at Beaufort Castle, near Inverness, as the guest of Lord and Lady Lovat. Maurice Baring would be there as well, and the two men would diligently sit down to their typewriters, while others shot the grouse or stalked the deer. In 1932, however, Beaufort Castle was let for the summer and, no alternative hospitality presenting itself, Ronald Knox was driven to renting a cottage at Rottingdean. It was something of a let-down. But if he could not write a book *at* Beaufort, he would write a book *about* Beaufort—and the result was *Sanctions*.

"Kingussie Castle" at once suggests the neighbourhood of Inverness, but it is with the tenants of the Castle, not with its owners, that the book is concerned. Let no one, therefore, try to discover in it the portraits of any living persons. We are simply told that the Kingussies (whom we never meet) are Catholic, and a priest arrives one morning to say Mass for the Catholic members of the household. There the resemblance to Beaufort ends, although the *cognoscenti* may like to guess at which twist or turning of the Beauly river this or that dialectical match is drawn. For Ronald Knox is too artistic to count his conversions before they are hatched. The idea of *Sanctions* was inspired by W. H. Mallock's *New Republic* where a number of guests, all distinguished by a high intellectual voltage, are invited to a house party where the problems of the universe shall be thrashed out. The book had been a minor Victorian classic, and Mallock had become a Catholic on his death-bed. *Sanctions* describes itself as a "frivolity"—perhaps a self-deprecating gesture intended to catch the frivolous reader by the coat-tails. It is, in fact, an intensely serious symposium. As an exhibition of dialectical swordsmanship, it shows Ronald Knox at his most agile; and—perhaps because he can hide beneath the multiple faces of fiction—it has a discursive playfulness and emotional depth, which he would hardly have allowed himself if he had been speaking in his own person.

The book is full of excellent and characteristic observation —as, for example, that "there are no villages in Scotland," only trim little towns; that "a pipe that refuses to draw just after breakfast is guilty of desertion in the face of the enemy"; that the beauties of a Scots garden "are the prize of the energetic. To visit it is an expedition, and a raid on its delphiniums best conducted by motor"; that "scenery spoils thought, and thought scenery"—except for dons who go for

the same walk every day. The *dramatis personae* have the
nicely calculated versatility of a Brains Trust, and they add
up to considerably more than their opinions. The most amusing, by far, is the Modernist Canon Oxenthorpe, to whom
Knox allows no quarter. Not since the Anglican Alphabet had
delighted the Anglo-Catholic *giovani* in those dear, dead days
when Jerusalem was being rebuilt in Graham Street[1] had
Ronald Knox so enjoyed himself at the expense of the Church
of England. Watch the infinitely liberal Canon greet the
Hungarian philosopher-*divorcé*:

> . . . the Canon's handshake with the Count was a masterpiece. It
> was accompanied by a look full of tactful understanding, meant
> to imply that the Canon knew all about the Count's unfortunate
> circumstances, and felt for him deeply; that, while he did not, of
> course, approve of his matrimonial arrangements, he was not
> going to be insular about them; brought up in a Latin country
> (all Catholics abroad were Latins to Canon Oxenthorpe) the
> Count was without the advantage of an intelligent religion, and
> therefore much must be excused.

Then there are the two Catholic converts—Mrs. Donovan,
"brought up in a strong family tradition of Agnosticism,
progress, and love of the Alps," and Chase, on whom the
burden of direct apologetic largely rests. He is strongly aided
by the Count (admirably drawn) who, one is pretty sure, will
end up on the right side, and by Lydiard, the intelligent
sceptic, who is asking for instruction when the party breaks
up. Escridge, the congenital progressive, might have drawn

[1] St. Mary's, Graham Street, a well-known Anglo-Catholic church in London, to which Knox had been attached in his Anglican days.

Ronald Knox's fire rather more sharply than in fact he does—but the most shattering broadsides are wisely reserved for Oxenthorpe. (It is difficult for Catholics to realize that in 1932 the pronouncements of Dr. Barnes were still being taken seriously by the semi-educated readers of the popular Press.) Perhaps Barton, the High Church clergyman, is the only symposiast who really fails to come alive; and his rôle is not an important one.

Like *Difficulties*, but more markedly, *Sanctions* has its period charm. A house party of this size and kind was still a plausible hypothesis. Gerald Chase tells his "man" to return a book he had run off with; in Mallock's day this would have been understood, but it was getting a little late, in 1932, for the average guest to have a "man." And the following reflections of Lydiard are an elegiac lament for a world—an age—whose limitations Ronald Knox understood as well as any, but many of whose achievements he admired and most of whose amenities he regretted:

We are like old men sitting by the river at the end of our journey, impatient for our burial, and for the little ransom that will take us to our own place. The feebleness of age has come upon us, we cannot tell how; it has stolen upon us while we slept, and left us no memories of our brave youth, and no treasure of experience. Our friends have left us, and the landmarks we had grown accustomed to, and it has all passed in a moment, like Rip Van Winkle's sleep, and left us dissatisfied with our youthful guesses, and cheated of the garnered wisdom that comes with years.

Controversy dates, but it dates charmingly in *Caliban in Grub Street* (1930). The adherence of so many powerful modern minds to the doctrines of the Catholic Church was a fact of life unknown to the popular *litterati* of the preceding decade. With other facts of life they were only too familiar. The theological relativism of *Foundations* had fathered a perfectly legitimate progeny in the moral relativism of Bertrand Russell and H. G. Wells. It was not the outlines of history alone that had become beautifully blurred. The study of the Synoptics had been succeeded by the study of the Symposiasts. People had listened to Canon Streeter's theory of the Resurrection because they supposed him to be an expert; they listened to the views of Mr. John Drinkwater and Mr. Hugh Walpole on similar subjects because they were subjects upon which these gentlemen professed no *expertise* whatever. A popular interest in religion is generally a sign of religious decay. Like democracy, family life, and Anglo-American relations, religion is all the healthier for not being ignorantly and incontinently discussed. A boom in religious sentiment often accompanies a slump in religious belief. The symposiasts —and they stretched from Miss Rebecca West to Mr. Hannen Swaffer—satisfied the public curiosity to know what So-and-So felt about God. There was little or no public desire to know whether, in fact, God existed; and whether, in fact, He had spoken.

All this was an invitation to Ronald Knox to display his swordsmanship—an invitation that, at the height of his powers, he was not tempted to resist. To say that he laid about him with a will would give too crude a picture of his finesse; you might as well have described Frank Woolley as smashing them to the boundary through the slips. But it would not be unfair to say that he enjoyed the bowling. The Symposiats were easier game, of course, than the Foundation Fathers; for one thing, they were not theologically educated. But Ronald Knox, like the good batsman that he was, treated them seriously, and he had more respect for some than for others. All of them represented some section of the public they had been called upon to entertain. Lord Russell had not yet acquired the status of a sage; yet he too was a target, although he was not yet a sitting target. Condescending to the readers of *Everyman,* he seemed to maintain that although it was enormously improbable that there should be any intelligent organisms in the Universe at all, it was quite probable there should be one or two. This did not seem to make sense to Ronald Knox. He understood what a busy man Lord Russell must be—but if he were going to write about religion, why could he not do so sensibly? He preferred, however, Lord Russell's contention that Christ was a megalomaniac to the more common Symposiast assumption that He was a man who never, by any chance, talked about Himself. It was quite easy, as Ronald Knox showed, to rewrite St. Matthew's Gospel in a way that buttressed this assumption; but it involved a great deal of cutting.

He preferred Arnold Bennett who had got as far as Kant to Hugh Walpole who had never got any further than Hugh Walpole's inner feelings. It was beyond his brief, perhaps, to point out that Arnold Bennett was the better novelist—and this was before Walpole's celebrated remark that he would deplore the spread of Catholicism because he thought it would be a bad thing for the novel. Knox knew too much about life and literature, not to mention theology, to confuse literary pleasure and mystical ecstasy: Keats was a great poet —as great as you like—but it was ridiculous to classify him with Plotinus and Augustine. Paradise and Parnassus may overlap—one hopes they do—but they are distinct localities. It was not easy to imagine Goethe saying: "Son, be of good cheer; thy sins be forgiven thee"; or Keats declaring: "A greater than Solomon is here." Miss Rebecca West liked going into Roman Catholic churches for the sake of the ritual, because the ritual drew a picture of spiritual facts which human language still found it difficult to express adequately. But when you got down to asking her what the facts were, or rudely suggesting that ritual was mumbo-jumbo unless it corresponded with reality, she replied, in effect, that the whole point of religion was that it had not been revealed; and that the fun of the game was finding it out for yourself. The simplicity of the Cross had given way to the complexity of a crossword puzzle—and to a *Times* crossword puzzle at that. This was all very well for Miss West; but for the kind of people to whom the Founder of Christianity had more particularly addressed Himself—fishermen, for example—it made the going difficult.

It was too much to hope that our old friend "outworn forms of creed and dogma" would not make its complacent reappearance, and here was a ball that Knox could hardly help but send spinning to the boundary. All these eminent authors were reacting against dogma, without having any notion of what dogma meant. They assumed that it derived from a Latin word meaning to teach, and that it was something imposed by crafty priests on the uncorrupted intelligence of mankind. In fact, the derivation was Greek; and the word meant that something had been agreed upon. None of the Symposiasts even asked themselves the question: why had so many people, for so many hundreds of years, agreed about certain things? The consensus of scientific opinion that the earth moved round the sun did not make that scientific fact automatically unacceptable—though appearances might suggest the contrary. The historical fact of the Resurrection might be improbable at first—or second—sight; the proofs brought forward in support of it might lack coercive force; but it was not made more improbable by the fact that millions of people agreed that it had happened.

Caliban in Grub Street was an answer—agile, witty, and not in the least ill-tempered—to what may be described as popular modernism; to what modernism had become by the time the dons had done with it. In trying to rescue an ethical Christ from the Christ of "the Churches," the Symposiasts had reduced to nonsense the Gospels to which they made their highly selective appeal, and the early Christian history of which they knew nothing whatever. "I believe" had indeed degenerated into "one does feel." Remark that there was little anyone could describe as revolutionary about the Symposiasts of the Rothermere Press. Marxism was hardly as yet on the literary map; the 'thirties still had their obsessions in store. There has not been a less revolutionary figure in English literature than Henry Arthur Jones, nor a safer Liberal than Arnold Bennett. The Athenaeum had no more reliable prop than genial Sir Hugh; and whoever may have unfurled a banner it was not Mr. Warwick Deeping. The Symposiasts were incorrigibly middle-class; and what they represented was not a middle-class revolution but a middle-class recoil. Only the single aristocrat among them—Bertrand Russell—would have openly proclaimed himself a Socialist, and did openly proclaim himself an atheist. For the most part they formed—and fed—the misty mentality of the Lending Libraries; and it was with this mentality, generally honest and generally uneducated, that Ronald Knox had now come to grips. Looking back to the days when he had exposed the instability of *Foundations*, he must have found it extraordinarily piquant that the only clergyman among his new opponents—the Reverend R. J. Campbell—had produced the most astonishing opinion of all; that the achievement of Lord Beaverbrook's ambitions was a proof of the efficacy of prayer. Mr. Campbell could not be certain that Lord Beaverbrook prayed to God; but no matter, he had prayed.

He sent forth his thought winged with energy, like a wireless beam-ray, into the invisible, and there were sent back to him in response the conditions he needed for the achievement of his aims.

No, for a Test Match cricketer, it had all been much too easy; only Bertrand Russell had proved a bowler worthy of Knox's bat, and even Russell had sent down a disappointingly large number of loose balls.

The new arena of broadcasting gave a priceless opportunity to the "omniscientists" to set the pattern of a kind of standard culture, which might soon become the quasi-official culture of the nation. Ronald Knox was well aware of the danger, and *Broadcast Minds* (1932) was an attack not upon anything that had actually been said over the air, but on the kind of thing that might be said over the air by the popular pundits of the day, if they were consistent with what they had already said in print. It was still necessary to counter the illusion that science and religion were irreconcilably opposed. The satire of *Reunion All Round* did not sound in the least far-fetched when Professor Julian Huxley seriously looked forward to a universal religion which should dispense with the belief in

God. This was about as sensible as looking forward to an era of universal aesthetic sensibility which should dispense with the appreciation of El Greco, or to a generation of hungry males with never a woman to satisfy them. The Christian religion is replete with mysteries, but nothing in it is more mysterious than Professor Huxley's determination not to have his cake and eat it. Still, Professor Huxley was at least a scientist—but what was Mr. H. L. Mencken? The name is all but forgotten, but in the early 'thirties it was still conjuring. Ronald Knox had no difficulty in proving that Mr. Mencken was an unconscious humorist. "To this day the wine used at the Eucharist is almost invariably red, not white"; "The Emperor Henry V crawling on his knees in the snows of Canossa"—these were among the jewels he had left lying about in his *Treatise on the Gods*. In his confusion of magic with religion Mencken had salted "the mines of pre-history by laying there, out of his own invention, the precise trail he wants us to find." There is always a certain excitement in a paper chase, but it does not conduct you to anything important. Knox observed that there was nothing remarkable in the resemblance between Tennyson's King Arthur and the Prince Consort because the character of the first was written round the character of the second. Mr. Mencken was an old hand at writing up parts for puppets, but for all that he was an inexcusably careless dramatist. "There was a time," he had written, "when a man laid low by the ague sent for a priest and made a votive offering; now he sends for a physician and takes quinine." He had forgotten that quinine was introduced into Europe by the Jesuits.

Next on the list came Mr. Gerald Heard with *The Emergence of Man* and a picture on the dust-jacket representing what Mr. P. G. Wodehouse had once described as "a fairly nude chappie giving the dawn the glad eye." The book was written before Mr. Heard had left to join the neocenobites on their Californian ranches. He was still in his Egyptian phase, and he looked to Ronald Knox as if he might well be about to "carve himself a niche in literature as the Guedalla of the early Pharaohs." Nor was Mr. Heard's eye so glad as all that; "Man," he exclaimed, "has emerged into inescapable ignorance." The fact did not depress him, since he was unconcerned with anything so trivial as individual human destinies. Man the Type—that was all that mattered. Ronald Knox replied that, to him, it mattered very little. "I do not see why men, real, living, concrete men, should have endured in every age a million agonies to give artistic satisfaction to Mr. Heard. Let us wish him a long life, that he may survive to see the next phase of human experience. I do not pretend to guess what it will be, but I cherish the certainty that it will give him, and all the prophets, a nasty jolt." It did; and, as we shall see, Ronald Knox was almost alone among the prophets to make any sense of the explosion.

Mr. Langdon-Davies—and here the name is hardly remembered at all—found it easy to dismiss religion by the following process of argument. Euclid was an old Greek, whose views Einstein had proved to be nonsense, and since Aristotle was another old Greek (no Greek had apparently ever been young) therefore his views must be nonsense too. Since Christianity was invented in the Middle Ages, when people thought a lot of Aristotle, therefore Christianity was founded on a false basis and must obviously be untrue. The triumphant corollary to be drawn from all this was that everyone could have as many wives as they liked, and all at the same time.

Easy game—though it is a little sad that Ronald Knox should have found it necessary to waste his time on it. When, however, he came to *The Prospects of Whelxleyanism*—Mr. Wells's *What Are We To Do With Our Lives?* and Professor Huxley's *What Dare I Think?*—he was at grips with sterner stuff. These men aimed at substituting a quite new culture for the culture which Europe had owned for nearly two thousand years; and the new culture would dispense with religion as religion had been understood and practised during that time. Mr. Wells, who was "an adept at being on the side of the big battalions," was prepared to tolerate religion, under appropriate safeguards, "as a kind of cocktail for the reformer." Without "the desire for service" which was among "the undying elements in every religious system," his Open Conspiracy would hardly gain the expected number of adherents.

Like any despairing incumbent, Mr. Wells was out to make his new religion popular; and it need hardly be added that he was out to make it efficient. By contrast, Professor Huxley, "aloof from the dust of these mundane conflicts," sat in his "expurgated oratory, contemplating, with occasional uprushes from his sub-conscious, a long row of statues—laws of nature on this side, human values on that." Who would join him at his orisons? What a pity that other rows of statues—on Chartres Cathedral, for example—drew a larger audience; statues for which even he would have liked somehow to find a place! Both Wells and Huxley were under the impression that a good Christian would make a good atheist. Ronald Knox hoped that they would be undeceived by failure, and he was certain they would be undeceived by success.

He left his most formidable antagonist to the last. Lord

Russell's antipathy to religion was a wish-fulfilment, because Lord Russell was a pessimist before he was a sceptic. Herein he stood opposed to Wells, Huxley and Heard. No contemporary eye was less glad than his. Yet Lord Russell was too faithful a servant of his mind not to recognize the good things of life when he saw them; and might he not have worked out from these recognitions a philosophy of Good to balance his philosophy of Evil? Might not this have left him free "to discuss, without prepossession, the major problems of theodicy"? Instead, he faced the future—as he still faces it—with the courage of unflinching despair. But it was "a grim Bible that has its Genesis torn out, and so discouraging an Apocalypse."

That was an end of controversy, and Ronald Knox—like other controversialists—must occasionally have wondered whether it had been worth while. He had used the weapon of laughter in addressing himself to people who could no longer laugh, and the weapon of reason in talking to people who could no longer think, and the weapon of knowledge in informing people who were indifferent to fact. And even if he had demolished the pundits, he had put up nothing in their place. That was the task of apologetics. His audience was the audience that listened to Chesterton—at its best, an educated but not an academic audience—and there were probably not a few dessicated intellectuals who discounted the arguments of a man who wrote so well, dared to dispense with footnotes, and used his erudition without parading it. Certainly, Ronald Knox, when he looked back on his years of controversy, was well aware that he had not pierced the sound-barrier. On one of the last occasions I saw him he showed me the manuscript of what purported to be the beginnings of a new apologetic.

This was published by *The Month*, after his death, with a Preface by Mr. Evelyn Waugh. After completing the second chapter he thought of recasting the whole work in the form of a conversation: here, as before, Mallock's *New Republic* would be his model. It was getting rather late, in 1956, to assemble his guests in a country-house; so he would assemble them on a "brains trust" instead. He sent the two versions of his second chapter to three friends, all of whom preferred his former method of direct exposition. He had already started on his third chapter when the translation of Ste. Thérèse's *Auto-biography* demanded his full attention, and the book of apologetics was never resumed. *Proving God* includes such portions of it as were found among his papers. They were never revised. Mr. Waugh tells us that Knox was explicitly dissatisfied with them and that he would never have published them precisely as they stand today. But they give us a tantalising glimpse of what might conceivably have been the most valuable book he ever wrote.

Compare *Proving God* with *Broadcast Minds* and you measure not only the distance between controversy and apologetics—between criticism and dialectic—but between the summer and autumn of a man's writing. The Ronald Knox of *Broadcast Minds* was exultantly self-confident; the Ronald Knox who sought to prove God when his sixty-ninth birthday was already past had learnt a great deal more about human beings, and something more, maybe, about God. The world was no longer divided between angels who agreed with him and devils who didn't. His opinions had even come to harmonise a little with the pattern of existing thought, and experience had "softened the hard edges of his affirmations." The aim of his apologetic was "not so much truth as reality."

He knew, of course, that the distinction was grossly unphilo-
sophical, but it expressed his awareness that the presentation
of the divine fact to the human mind called for persuasion,
and that if you would persuade you must study the working
of other people's minds. Here experience was an indispensable
guide, and that is why what Ronald Knox described as "an
old man's book" was so eminently worth the writing—
though it did not set out to be more than a suggestion for the
book which he hoped one day would be written by someone
better qualified than himself. Call it the summary for a
Summa and you have pretty clearly grasped its scope.

The sequence of detached considerations, which is all we
possess, hung on the thread of a single criticism—that most
Catholic apologetic strikes the modern reader as inhuman.
"Just because it is worked out with such mathematical precision, just because a suitable answer comes pat to every question, just because it always seems to face you with a dilemma
from which there is no logical escape, it afflicts our contemporaries with a sense of *malaise*." This was a bitter pill for the
Seminary professors to swallow; but whereas it might be useful to talk the language of rationalism to an age of reason,
were there not signs that we were living in an age of will? If
so, might not Pascal command attention where St. Thomas
did not? Ronald Knox did not question the necessity for intellectual propaganda; he only thought that the effect of intellectual protest was spoilt by isolation "from that moral and
spiritual witness which, as Christians, we do not cease to
bear." This had opened up a dangerous cleavage between
those who affirmed that you could not know God by reason,
and therefore it was useless to make the attempt, and those
who affirmed that if you did not know God by reason you

could not know him at all. In both versions of his second chapter Knox argued that, at its highest, man's apprehension of God is conjointly (not simultaneously) the work of his intellect and of his will. If you seasoned the lucidity of St. Thomas with the unction of Pascal, and based your proof of God's existence on St. Thomas' argument from contingent being, you committed no sin against philosophical honesty. The faculties of heart and mind were like the two lobes of the brain and should, by rights, function as smoothly. "In practice, they have to be stimulated alternately—and by a single process, because the recognition of our own inadequacy as creatures is at once the guarantee of God's existence and the basis of all worship."

Most readers will agree that the attempt to gather the disputants round the microphone was a mistaken one. It belonged to another book and harked back to an earlier phase of Ronald Knox's writing. He could no longer enjoy himself so light-heartedly at other people's expense, and even his accurate characterization of the Question Master strikes a note of triviality which is felt, here, to be out of key. We want Ronald Knox to speak to us in his own person, not in the French accent of Monsieur Deschamps—and so, no doubt, he would have spoken if he had lived to finish the book. As it is, we are left questioning the absolute of time: an idea that the writers of scientific fiction might easily have played with, but for all that, "Can we really imagine a Creator so tied up in His own machine that it would be impossible for Him to reverse in fact what his creatures can reverse in fancy? However much imagination boggles at the idea of a Supreme Being who is outside time, common sense revolts from the idea of one who is subject to its limitations . . ."

The three dots which close this fascinating fragment recall the uncompleted edifice of Pascal, and the *pensées* of Ronald Knox were too deep and searching to be contained by the slick formulas of the schools. It was only by continuing to ask the questions that the faint and wavering shadows of an answer might be cast on the blank spaces of the mind by the sunrays of the Divine intelligence. In the fullness of time, Time's secrets would be yielded up, and Ronald Knox had not long to wait.

In an interesting but elusive short story, *The Reprieve*, also published in *The Month* (December 1956) Ronald Knox reverted to the method of symposium. A small group of dons and scientists are dining just outside the protective barbed wire of Harwell Atomic Energy station. We shall see later on what Ronald Knox thought about atomic energy; here he sets the old argument about the use of force circulating on its well-oiled wheels. The scientist who has only, supposedly, to press a button in order to destroy the world boasts that he will have no compunction in doing so if he thinks the world will be the better for coming to an end. His interlocutor retires to bed and has a curious dream in which he sees the *bambino* in the familiar shape of a Donatello plaque thrown like a shadow on the back of his hand. From that moment on he sees the *bambino* everywhere, until it gives him the impression of ownership. The dream turns presently into a nightmare. His atomic friend is driving him along a narrow road, with high walls on either side, so that it gave him the sensation of a tunnel, and he keeps on saying, "Bought with a price! It isn't yours!" But the scientist drives faster and faster until they come to a road sign on which the *bambino* is painted in red against a white background. He jams on the brakes and the sleeper wakes up before they crash their heads into the windscreen.

Discussing the dream next morning, the scientist suggests that his proposal to destroy the world had perhaps struck his friend as a kind of trespassing.

"Desecration would be a better word, I think . . . You know, in my dreams I always find myself taken back over a space of fifteen or twenty years; the places I frequent are places which have long ceased to be familiar, the friends I consort with are men now among the dead. And perhaps the dreamer of last night was not myself as I am now, but myself as I was twenty years ago, when I wasn't much more than a boy, and believed firmly in much that now seems doubtful. It might have been a young man's vision; it is only an old man's dream. And I don't expect you to be guided by it."

"Oh, as to that," comes the reply, "well, you see, the question doesn't arise . . . because of course I was only pulling your leg."

It is true that in the concluding paragraph of the story the scientist wonders whether his friend has really had the dream, and the friend wonders whether the scientist was really pulling his leg. But if the limited possibility of a reprieve has been opened up, it is because time has stopped for a moment and redemption is actual and immediate. Masbury—the friend—must not be read as a personification of Ronald Knox. He is a composite image, rather, of modern man not quite sold to a desperate determinism, and with memories longer than he realises. In the great existential debate of the twentieth century it was still possible that the *bambino* would have the last word.

That it would have the last word of all Ronald Knox never

doubted for an instant, and he faced, once again in *The Month* (1950), the classical difficulty about the Second Coming. St. Paul had written that the appearance of Antichrist would be the necessary prelude to this, and had suggested that some influence was holding Antichrist in check. Knox agreed with Père Prat that this was a superhuman agency, but what did St. Paul mean by its being "cleared out of the way"? Knox, with his exegete's eye, suggested that the verb should be taken intransitively; i.e. the power in question rather than actively hindering was passively "holding back." And supposing this neutralizing force were the incredulity of Israel, creating a kind of bottle-neck? Might not the first Christians have believed, as Christians still believe, that the Second Coming must wait on the conversion of Israel, although the appearance of Antichrist would intervene between the one event and the other? And when Our Lord had prophesied that "this generation will not have passed, before all this is accomplished," He had meant not only the threat of the Roman armies to Jerusalem, but also the return of Christ in judgment —if all went well. But all had not gone well, and the prospect was deferred. This was Ronald Knox's guess, and he made it in all diffidence. It showed, nevertheless, how deeply, in these last years of his life, the consummation of time which had never been far absent from his mind had taken hold of his imagination.

8

THE TRANSLATOR

THIS WAS THE LAST and perhaps the most imposing image that Ronald Knox left upon the face of English letters; it was not necessarily the most important. In 1939 he was commissioned by the Hierarchy to produce a new Translation of the Bible, which was later sanctioned for use in Catholic churches throughout England and Wales. For a long time the English Catholics had been in a difficulty about the Bible. The Douai *émigrés* had produced a vigorous translation which some competent judges—Professor Phillimore among them— thought superior even to the Authorised Version. Then Bishop Challoner in the eighteenth century had revised this— smoothed it out would be a more exact description—to make it read a little more like most people by then imagined the Bible to be. Thus the original Douai translation became for all practical purposes inaccessible. What was generally known as the "Douay" version, read in Parish churches up and down the country, was not the Douai version at all. When I was rehearsing Dorothy Sayers' sequence of radio plays, *The Man Born To Be King*, an Irish member of the cast remarked to me: "These plays are very interesting to me, because we Catholics are not allowed to read the Bible." It was not an instructed remark, but it disclosed the gap that Ronald Knox was called upon to fill between the Protestants who knew the Bible at the expense of the Church and the Catholics who hardly knew it at all.

The Knox Bible was an immense achievement, and it is difficult for anyone brought up on the Authorised Version, and made to learn the Collects by heart in Cranmer's incomparable prose, to discuss it fairly. Once you have got "Prevent us, O Lord, in all our doings" into your head, it is only of academic interest to be told that "prevent" means to "go before" —even if that was not the meaning you had attached to the word when it first became lodged in your memory. Ronald Knox must have found the same difficulty in expelling these hallowed cadences from his ear. Even when people become Catholics, they very often continue to read the Bible in the Authorised Version, as Newman did to the end of his life— although that is one of the facts about Newman which is not commonly stressed. But Knox was translating for people who had little or no acquaintance with the Authorised Version, and who for the most part only knew the Challoner-Douay when they were compelled to listen to it in church. If an old-fashioned Bible reader found that he had rendered it more exactly, so much the better. But these were not, principally, the people he was aiming at.

He was working, all the time, under close ecclesiastical supervision, and it was not long—as he told us at the Hyde Park Hotel—before he learnt what it meant "to take correction from earthly Fathers." I am not competent to discuss his translation from a doctrinal or linguistic point of view, and on both he had as much advice as he could comfortably digest. I am only concerned to discuss the Knox Bible as literature. For my own part, I wish that he had been asked to revise the Authorised Version in accordance with Catholic doctrine and modern scholarship, with his own commentary at hand to clear up obscurities, so that the Bible read by Catholics should be as like as possible to the Bible read by Anglicans. I believe that nothing else would have so helped English Christians to feel as one. The power of Anglicanism has always been, to a very large extent, the power—the incantatory power, if you like—of great prose. If Catholics were encouraged to draw upon this power—and if they were allowed to take a leaf or two out of *Hymns Ancient and Modern* and *The English Hymnal*—it might help them to feel more English, and it might help Anglicans to feel more Catholic. But these are private longings—the wistful nostalgia of a convert. What Ronald Knox had been asked to do was to produce a Bible in modern dress. He must be judged by how far his intentions were sound and by how far his achievement lived up to them.

To begin with, his Bible must be original. It must be as unmistakably his as Tyndale's Bible and Coverdale's had been theirs. It must speak to the twentieth century as those had spoken to the sixteenth. It must discover its own rhythms and its own phraseology. Now, in the matter of translation, it is much easier to be original when you are the first, or among the first, in the field. But Knox had to turn his back on the whole literary idiom of English-speaking Christianity; to forget the accumulated associations of three centuries; and create something in tune with the modern ear—even if it was not in tune with the modern mind. And the trouble was that where

poetry was in question—and much of the Bible is poetry—
Ronald Knox did not really have an ear for modern literary
idioms. In that, as in so much else, he was a pre-1914 man. I
make bold to say that the Knox Bible would have been a far
more exciting literary achievement if it had been written by
Father Martindale. Realising perhaps that he was not really a
"modern," Knox deliberately tried to write in a style of what
he called "timeless" English—a kind of back-kneed genuflec-
tion to the enduring spell of the Authorised Version, which,
try as he might, he could not quite conjure away. Where the
translation fails—and again I speak only from the literary
standpoint—it fails for this reason. The trouble is not in the
least that it is modern, but that it is not modern enough; that
here, for once, Ronald Knox is not playing his own literary
game.

There does seem to have been a certain contradiction between Knox's aim and his retrospect. He did not, when he
looked back on his work, anticipate that it would defy the
passage of time, as the Authorised Version had so long defied
it. "All I ask of you," he told us at the Hyde Park Hotel, "is
to scrap the Knox Bible altogether when it has served its purpose." We were not to keep it like a suit of clothes that no
longer fits, or—he might have added—like a favourite pipe
that no longer draws as it used to. Meanwhile, however, there
it is—an integral furnishing of the English Catholic Establishment. The New Testament was translated and published
first. This was natural because people read the New Testament who rarely, or never, read the Old: and it is generally
the New Testament which is read aloud to them in Church.
In one respect, at least, the Knox Bible was timely. The very
splendour of the Authorised Version had begotten a superfi-

cial cult of the Bible "as literature," which was bad literary
criticism as well as bad exegesis. No great literature is literature and nothing else; it was senseless to read Isaiah as poetry
unless you also read him as prophecy. Knox's eschewal of the
sonorous phrase and the swelling rhythm forced the reader to
bend his whole attention to the matter in hand; and if the
manner were no more than serviceable, that might be all to
the good.

Nevertheless, the Bible is much more than a book; it is a
collection of books on very diverse subjects by very different
authors. Heaven knows, there is variety in Shakespeare, but
the difference in style, subject and mentality between *Love's
Labour Lost* and *The Tempest* is nothing like so great as the
difference between the Book of Genesis and the Epistle to the
Hebrews. The translator must rediscover in his own language
the idioms of poetry and prophecy, narrative and parable,
argument and symbolism. He must imitate the tone of voice in
which a man will tell a story, recount a vision, or write a
letter. The Authorised Version had been translated by a
committee at a moment when English prose had suddenly
reached a maturity so contagious that you could not tell when
one member of the committee had left off and another had
taken over. Ronald Knox was an immensely versatile man, but
he was not as versatile as all that; and when Father Martindale
asked him how he would differentiate between the style of St.
Paul and the style of St. John, he replied that he would not
differentiate between them at all. It was a rather damaging
admission.

I shall shock no one if I suggest that the Gospels and Epistles alike bristle with difficulties, and it is the first business of
the translator or the exegete to clear them up without hushing
them up. Let us see how far Knox went towards solving

them. What sense, for example, does he make of the Parable of the Unjust Steward? He must often have seen the look of collective bewilderment on the faces of a congregation as they listened to the familiar words regularly, reverently, and un-comprehendingly read out to them. Here are the words of the Vulgate, from which he was translating:

Et laudavit dominus villicum iniquitatis, quia prudenter fecisset: quia filii huius saeculi prudentiores filiis lucis in generatione sua sunt. Et ego vobis dico: facite vobis amicos de mammona iniquitatis: it, cum defeceritis, recipiant vos in aeterna tabernacula.

Here the Authorised Version gives us:

And the Lord commended the unjust steward, because he had done wisely: for the children of this world are in their generation wiser than the children of light. And I say unto you, Make to yourselves friends of the Mammon of unrighteousness; that, when ye fail, they may receive you into everlasting habitations.

The Challoner-Douay only varies this by substituting "for as much as" for "because," and "dwellings" for "habitations." We are no nearer a solution. Now listen to Knox:

And this knavish steward was commended by his master for his prudence in what he had done; for indeed, the children of this world are more prudent after their own fashion than the children of the light. And my counsel to you is, make use of your base wealth to win yourselves friends, who, when you leave it behind, will welcome you into eternal habitations.[1]

[1] *The Holy Bible*, tr. Ronald Knox. Copyright 1944, 1948, 1950 Sheed & Ward, Inc., N.Y.; quoted by permission of the Cardinal Archbishop of Westminster.

It is already much clearer. "Prudence" has taken the place of "wisdom"; "base wealth" explains "Mammon"; and there is a touch of real originality in translating "*defeceritis*" by "leaving behind." Yet the dress is still not quite modern. Why not "scamp" instead of "knavish," "in their own way" for "after their own fashion," "advice" for "counsel," and—let us say— "the mansions of eternity" for "eternal habitations"? Try as he may to forget them, the old phrases ring in the translator's memory.

Now take a passage of plain narrative: the account of the Nativity in St. Luke's Gospel:

And Joseph also went up from Galilee, out of the city of Nazareth, into Judaea, unto the city of David, which is called Bethlehem; (because he was of the house and lineage of David) to be taxed with Mary his espoused wife, being great with child. And so it was that while they were there, the days were accomplished that she should be delivered. And she brought forth her first-born son, and wrapped him in swaddling clothes, and laid him in a manger; because there was no room for them in the inn.

Here is Knox:

And Joseph, being of David's clan and family, came up from the town of Nazareth, in Galilee, to David's city in Judaea, the city called Bethlehem, to give in his name there. With him was his espoused wife Mary, who was then in her pregnancy; and it was while they were still there that the time came for her delivery. She brought forth a son, her first-born, whom she wrapped in his swaddling-clothes, and laid in a manger, because there was no room for them in the inn.

Here there is nothing remarkable about the Authorised Version, except the facts which it records, and Challoner-Douay differs from it in no material respect. Knox, it is true, gives us one or two sensible modernisms; but once again, the question asks itself—is this how a good modern writer would recount these particular happenings? Ronald Knox had an excellent sense of rhythm—he wrote aloud, so to speak—but here he seems to be writing to a rhythm which is not his own. Would a contemporary writer say "brought forth" rather than "give birth to," and would he not say simply "pregnant" rather than "in her pregnancy"? Sir Arnold Lunn, in a very acute criticism[2] of Knox's translation, has drawn attention to the many places where he has impaired both sense and rhythm by unnecessary verbal additions. A tone of voice which was natural to the early seventeenth century has acquired an accent of affected reverence—an accent which Ronald Knox, when he was writing or speaking in his own person, so well knew how to avoid.

Knox's translation of the Magnificat shows the full extent of his failure. Compare the compulsive rhythm of the Authorised and Douay versions—they differ hardly at all:

My soul doth magnify the Lord, and my spirit hath rejoiced in God my Saviour. For he hath regarded the low estate of his handmaiden: for behold, from henceforth all generations shall call me blessed. For he that is mighty has done to me great things; and holy is his name.

with Knox's modernisation:

[2] See *And Ever New.*

My soul magnifies the Lord; my spirit has found joy in God, who is my Saviour, because he has looked graciously upon the lowliness of his handmaid. Behold, from this day forward all generations will count me blessed; because he who is mighty, he whose name is holy, has wrought for me his wonders.

Poetry has been turned into prose by needless transpositions and the loss of a few syllables; and in these matters a miss is as good as a mile. It is not enough to change "henceforth" to "from this day forward" to bring the passage up to date. The new translation is at once too like the old, and not like enough.

It is generally conceded that Knox was at his best in translating St. Paul, because in the case of St. Paul the intellect is more important than the ear. It matters immensely that we should know what St. Paul was talking about. The purple passages, it is true, lose their spell; you cannot set "I may speak with every tongue that men and angels use; yet, if I lack charity, I am no better than echoing bronze, or the clash of cymbals" against "Though I speak with the tongues of men and of Angels, and have not charity, I am become as sounding brass, or a tinkling cymbal." Here St. Paul's meaning is clear, and we are brought no nearer to it. But what is the mere layman to make of the following passage from the Epistle to the Romans?

What shall we say then? Is the law sin? God forbid. Nay, I had not known sin, but by the law: for I had not known lust, except the law had said, "Thou shalt not covet." But sin, taking occasion by the commandment, wrought in me all manner of concupiscence. For without the law sin was dead. For I was alive without the law once; but when the commandment came, sin revived, and

I died. And the commandment, which was ordained to life, I found to be unto death. For sin, taking occasion by the commandment, deceived me, and by it slew me. Wherefore the law is holy, and the commandment holy, and just, and good. (A.V.)

Let us now see what admirable sense Ronald Knox makes of the same passage:

Does this mean that law and guilt are the same thing? God forbid we should say that. But it was only the law that gave me my knowledge of sin; I should not even have known concupiscence for what it is, if the law had not told me, Thou shalt not covet. But the sense of sin, with the law's ban for its foothold, produced in me every sort of concupiscence. Without the law, the sense of sin is a dead thing. At first, without the law, I was alive; then, when the law came with its ban, the sense of sin found new life, and with that, I died. The ban, which was meant to bring life, proved death to me; the sense of sin, with the law's ban for its foothold, caught me unawares, and by that means killed me. The law, to be sure, is something holy; the ban is holy, and right, and good.

St. Paul's argument is not easy, and Ronald Knox does not burke its complexity. But here, at last, he has found his idiom; here he really does seem to be writing as if he were removing a difficulty for Sir Arnold Lunn. Where the Bible appears to be plain sailing, I doubt very much whether readers will gain anything but incidental accuracies from Knox's version, and these will hardly compensate them for the rhetoric—and also the realism—which have been deliberately sacrificed. They may ask whether "timeless" English is not a half-way house to "basic" English—and "basic" English is no more than a convenience for those who cannot, or will not, learn a foreign language. The truth of the matter is that the translation of the Bible demanded a more adventurous literary talent than Ronald Knox possessed, if it were to take rank as literature. But to this criticism—which many people will contest—his version of the Epistles is a brilliant exception. Here, his service to Christian spirituality and biblical scholarship alike can hardly be exaggerated; and he could have rendered it without spending ten valuable years of his life on a task for which, in some respects, he showed himself to be not perfectly suited.

The judgment reads harshly, even impertinently, as I set it down: and it stands under correction. Ronald Knox knew very well what he was about. His last public appearance, appropriately enough, was in Oxford to deliver the Romanes Lecture on "English Translation." He had dragged himself, with difficulty and high courage, from a sick bed, and he gave his lecture sitting down. Many of his listeners knew that he was a dying man, and this was something that he had wanted, desperately, to do. He never did anything better. Compare this lecture (reprinted in *Literary Distractions*) with his unpublished lectures on Virgil, and you will find the same verve and wit, the same scholarship, the same alert intelligence, the same dexterity in argument, and the same felicity of phrase. You will also find the same evidence of hard work—for although Ronald Knox was never ponderous, he was never, even on the lightest occasion, superficial. "According to a recent paragraph in the newspapers, translators who are members of the Institute of Linguists have decided to increase their charges"—it was an easy opening.

Few Romanes lecturers have worn their blue ribbon with such insouciance. But listen to him as he gets down to business, boldly maintaining that a translation should be literary before it is literal, and that whatever idiom the translator chooses to work in, he must somehow get into the skin of his original. He must not confuse a translation with a crib. He goes on to make two important points about the Authorised Version of the Bible; first that the only great writer to have modelled a translation upon it was Milton in his rendering of Horace's Ode to Pyrrha—with quite disastrous results; and secondly, that the Authorised Version was not really a Jacobean version at all, but a Jacobean revision of an Elizabethan forerunner—Coverdale. If James I had set Donne, Herbert, Crashaw and other of their contemporaries to work on the Scriptures, the result would have been very different. I do not know whether Ronald Knox had ever read T. S. Eliot on Milton—whether, indeed, he had read T. S. Eliot on anything—but he does here seem to be in accord with Eliot's view that both Milton and the Authorised Version are eccentric in their use of language, and that their influence upon English literature has been, on the whole, a bad one. And so he takes us on a lightning tour of the English translators— translating, most of them, from Latin or Greek—pointing out the sea-change that has come over Chaucer and Virgil by the time that Dryden has done with them; seeing how Dr. Rieu has succeeded with Homer where T. E. Lawrence had not; submitting to the seventh wave which will always wash the translator overboard; but stressing—as Belloc, also lecturing at Oxford, had stressed in his Taylorian lecture—the importance of translation as an art, or even as a craft, at a time when the classics were rapidly losing their claim to be considered as a common language, even among educated people. It was not too much to say that the unity of European culture now depended, very largely, on the translator's skill. "Oh for a timeless English!" he exclaims. Odd that he should not have seen that, in the nature of history and language, there could never be any such thing.

He did not, however, stop at translating the Bible. One of the very last things he wrote was his translation of the *Autobiography of St. Thérèse of Lisieux*.[3] It was badly needed. When Catholics get hold of a good thing, they generally do their best to spoil it; and the people who ask Ste. Thérèse for her prayers would do well to ask for her forgiveness. Her physical likeness had been deformed by faked photographs and plaster statues of repellent sentimentality; her humility had been mocked by a pretentious basilica; and, worse, her writings had been edited by pious hands for the benefit of pious ears. Ronald Knox, working from the facsimile edition of her *Life*, at last enabled us to see her as she really was—in her heroism as well as in her humility, in her strength as well as in her tenderness. It is a moving thought that this elderly scholar, so remote from the ambience of the *petite bourgeoisie* —and nothing else about Ste. Thérèse was in the least *petit*— should have been able to get so completely inside her habit. With extraordinary tact he finds the English equivalent for her unadorned and unselfconscious style. How easily, if she had been writing in English, might she have referred to the "primrose path"; she would have remembered just enough Shakespeare for that, although she might well have forgotten by then that the phrase was Shakespeare's. Notice both the risk and avoidance of whimsey in the following passage:

[3] New York: Kenedy, 1959.

Children learn the secret of holiness—that is, the song of divine love—from those who are entrusted with their education just as birds learn to sing by listening to the parent bird. I had a canary once that sang to perfection; and at the same time I had a linnet which I tended with great care because I'd taken charge of it before it could fly. Born to captivity, it had no parents to learn from; but when it heard the canary trilling all day, it tried to follow suit. Not easy for a linnet; his gentle voice wasn't up to the shrill notes of his music-master. It was touching to witness his efforts, but they succeeded in the end; without losing the sweetness of his voice, he sang in canary fashion. Dear Mother, it was you who taught me to sing, from childhood upwards, it was your voice that thrilled me; and it's splendid, nowadays, to hear people say that I remind them of you! Not that I'm in the least like you really; but I do hope, with all my disabilities, to join my song with yours in eternity.

It would seem a little absurd to speak of a meeting of minds between Ronald Knox and Ste. Thérèse of Lisieux; but the meeting of souls is unmistakeable.

9

THE PREACHER

IN NOTHING WAS RONALD KNOX more professional than in his preaching. Most of the sermons he preached as a Catholic have been assembled by Fr. Philip Caraman, S.J., in two volumes under the titles *Pastoral* and *Occasional*. In a perceptive introduction to the first, Fr. Caraman compares the total body of Knox's teaching from the pulpit to Newman's Oxford Sermons; equal to these in scope and brilliance, and more valuable to the average modern reader because they are couched in a modern idiom and designed to answer modern difficulties. Knox had an extraordinary knack of taking the question out of your mouth, and at the same time reminding you of what you had forgotten to put into it. The Eucharist was, of course, at the centre of his religious thought and practice. When he began to doubt the validity of his Anglican Orders, he constantly asked himself whether anything was really "happening" at the altar. "I had to set my teeth to consecrate and make my thanksgiving after communion or confession with a mental reservation."[1] Most Catholics, when they approach the altar, are conscious only of communion with Christ; they forget that they are entering into communion

[1] Evelyn Waugh, *Monsignor Ronald Knox,* © Evelyn Waugh, 1959 (Boston: Little, Brown and Company), p. 145.

with each other. Ronald Knox reminded them that Holy Communion is pre-eminently the Sacrament of charity. How was it possible—people often asked—that God should care individually for the milling, anonymous, and generally unappealing crowds that meet us in the street: "faces hardened by money-getting, faces impudent with the affectation of vice, faces vacant with frivolity, faces lined with despair." Because the Eucharist was universally applicable, it was easier for us to imagine, and to imitate, the universality of the divine love.

Ronald Knox had a realistic appreciation of the contemporary mood. The generation he was addressing was not necessarily worse than those preceding it: it had its virtues as well as its vices. But it was "a careless generation, which has grown up with very little attention to the advice of its elders and, to tell the truth, somewhat in reaction from them. It has discarded conventions without replacing them by principles; it is apt to mistake excitement for happiness, passion for love, and eccentricity for genius. And it is very easy for Catholics, much easier than they know, to be carried away by it." And so, in preaching about marriage, Knox extolled the freedom of bondage; and in preaching about modesty, he justified the wisdom of restraint. The Christian life was an adventure, but it was not a rash adventure. Its perfection lay in self-sacrifice, not in self-indulgence—not even in self-expression. The crucifix stood in stark opposition to the humanist ideal. "When Jesus Christ entered heaven before you, His side was wounded, and His hands and feet were scarred." He had realised all the possibilities of his mission, but his life had been the reverse of what the world regards as a "life fully lived." Natural inclinations, even the most ardent natural affections, might have to be sacrificed for a greater, a supernatural, good.

It is not for a layman to analyse the coherence, rigour, and persuasiveness of Ronald Knox's pastoral teaching: it is sufficient to point them out. What concerns us here is the art with which they were applied. Note, for example, once again his skill in sustaining a comparison:

We are poor, we Catholics; it is easy for people to keep out of our way and pretend that they do not see us. Yet we make many rich; in those ugly, angular convents you see a cross on a gable, a name on a door-plate, easily overlooked—what lives have been spent in a pure activity of prayer! And we share that beneficent influence. There are financiers inside these secluding walls who deal in a currency the world does not dream of putting into circulation, by whispered prayers and muttered aspiration, that golden stream of grace that floats our souls' enterprises, when we think that our own credit is carrying us through. One bank looks very much like another from the outside; you cannot tell from the front windows whether it is doing good business. One religion looks very much like another from the outside; we cannot see yet what is happening behind the counters. But it is to us that Our Lord, by impoverishing Himself, has left the true capital to trade with.

Ronald Knox never lost himself in abstraction; he always brings you back to time and place. It was not enough for him that Our Lord was led up on to a high mountain; he must try to give it a name. Perhaps it was Mount Carmel, looking down on to the plain of Esdraelon, where East and West had so often met in conflict, and looking seawards to where the grain ships steered a northward course on their way from Alexandria to Rome. Ronald Knox, though he was himself so reluctant to cross the channel, had a vivid sense of historical movement—its abrupt changes and its recurring rhythms. Because he breathed antiquity like a native air, he could imagine the Gospels, as well as preach them. He could make a shrewd guess as to how the first rumours of Pentecost would strike a Hellenised Jew like St. Paul, or the squabbles of the Sanhedrin a sophisticated pro-consul like Pontius Pilate. The opening of a temporary chapel for the Oxford undergraduates in 1948 reminded him of the wattle huts where Aidan and Chad had said their Masses, and of which no relic remained. Mankind was entering a tunnel, and it was no time for Gothic grandeurs. Heathendom was at the gates; let an age of quiet reflection and common intellectual agreement bequeath its legacies of graceful stone. Ronald Knox asked his listeners to imagine

some remote ancestor of ours watching on the cliffs near Dover, the last dying camp-fire which the Roman legions had left burning to cover the evacuation of the province. He thought of those flames, perhaps, as the beacon-light of a new liberty. In fact he was contemplating the funeral-pyre of a great world-order. All the old landmarks were to be lost, all the tradition that had civilised us was to be buried; laboriously, for several centuries to come, Europe would be engaged in trying to build up, somehow, a new fabric of culture out of the ruins. And Britain, so remote and so defenceless, would experience to the full that time of distress. Religion, the law, the arts, the amenities of life, would have to be learnt again as from the beginning.

The cadences, and the feeling also, carry an echo of Newman; and indeed many of Knox's *Occasional Sermons* are worthy to be set beside Newman's *Sermons for Special Occasions*. Each man could enter into the spirit of a particular celebration—a beginning, or an end, or an anniversary. Each was intensely and poetically English; one of those "strange folk that live between the Severn and the Wash, between the Tweed and the English Channel; a folk honest, on the whole, kindly, on the whole, shy, a little surly, law-abiding, but doggedly tenacious of their rights, rather too self-satisfied, incurably sentimental, dreadfully muddle-headed." St. George—whose Feast occasioned these reflections—was the patron of "that country of chalk downs, of little fields bordered by green hedges, of wandering lanes, of hills scarcely rising above the level of cultivation, of old trees and of long manorial tenure, which we call England."

Set this beside another sermon preached on St. George's Day (April 23) 1915, at St. Silas', Kentish Town, a very "advanced" Anglo-Catholic church in the north of London. It was published later by the Ss. Peter and Paul Press, and its tone is rather more polemical than the preacher's sermons generally were. The voice is the voice of an *enfant terrible* deliberately raised to scare the complacencies of the hour. Knox had no doubt that the Allied cause was just—"thank God our hands are clean"—but then neither had anyone else, save for a few exceptions among whom he would have blushed to be included. The idea that England could ever be anything but a "top-class nation" would not have entered his head. He began by pointing out that April 23rd was also the Feast of St. Adalbert, a German saint who could not, however, possibly be suspected of assisting German arms. Knox had already got from Belloc the notion that the war was against Prussia, although Austria had provoked it—and Prussia was "a country, thanks to the Reformation, scarcely less heathen than when St. Adalbert found it." Nevertheless, England was a "nation with a dead soul," and the need of the moment was not only for men and munitions but for penance.

Now that doesn't mean that we're all to go about, as we've all been going about these last six months, suggesting various ways in which, instead of mortifying ourselves, we might contrive to mortify one another. It doesn't mean that we can satisfy our consciences by giving up horse-racing, or giving up intoxicating liquors, or giving up Gibraltar . . . The national curse is not drink, as the newspapers say. It is not hypocrisy, as the Germans say. The national curse is the national rejection of the Christian faith.

This, at least, is very much how the star performer of so many Catholic pulpits might have put it thirty years later. The Catholic Church in England, when he found his way to it, seemed to him "a little walled garden," fulfilling the promise of its Second Spring, and "enriched, not seldom, by windfalls from next door." It could not do without the windfalls, although Ronald Knox, like other English Catholics, may not always have appreciated their flavour. Yet Knox understood how the Englishry of the English had come to prejudice them against Catholicism, a prejudice whose sentimental depths only an Englishman—be he Protestant or Catholic—can understand. The English mind was "the slave of the *fait accompli*" and nothing had "contributed more successfully to the vogue of Anglicanism than its architectural connection with the past." It was that which made St. Etheldreda's, Ely Place, such a valuable exception. Here, ever since the 'seventies, Catholic Londoners had been able to hear Mass where the Bishops of Ely had celebrated it from the thirteenth century till the Reformation. And when Ronald Knox turned his mind to the old recusant families, like the Welds at Lulworth, they reminded him of cricketers, with no hope of victory, "who play out the innings for a draw."

He always appealed to the imagination of his listeners, but much more rarely to their emotions, because he knew that emotions do not last. Nevertheless he was capable, on occasion, of a rare descriptive eloquence. No preacher of the seventeenth century, which was the golden age of pulpit oratory, could have bettered the following passage:

Imagine yourself standing and looking into the tomb of Our Lord Jesus Christ, just before Nicodemus and Joseph rolled the stone into its place at the entrance to it. The sacred body is swathed in cerecloths; but you can see the outlines of it, and remember what it was this morning. Those feet, which now lie so still, were treading only this morning the painful road to Calvary; these three years past, they have worn themselves out on the roads of Judaea and Galilee, as He went about doing good. Those hands, now spread out motionless, were quick with life; nay, imparted life, radiated it, as Jairus' daughter and the young man at Nain and Lazarus could tell you. In the lines about the mouth, you can trace where He smiled in pardoning the penitent sinner; the brow was furrowed with anxious bewilderment over Jewish unbelief. All that frame, till this morning, was full of vitality; it belonged to one who never seemed to give Himself any rest, who prayed at night on lonely hillsides, and slept from sheer exhaustion amid the perils of a storm-swept lake. And now it lies quite still; God has finished His redemptive work, as He finished His creative work centuries ago, and He is hallowing the Sabbath day afresh; God rests, with the most perfect repose of all—the repose of death.

It is magnificent, and deeply moving—one can imagine with what violence and vulgarity another, more demagogic, preacher might have attempted to re-create the scene. Knox's prose has, here, the still beauty and exact workmanship of an Italian or a Flemish *pietà*. The familiar and the sublime, the melancholy and the majestic, are mingled with an artist's cunning. Yet the speaker's sincerity, even in cold print, removes all sense of contrivance; the signature of Ronald Knox is written all over it. But there are other sermons which are even more unmistakably his, because they are composed on themes which he was especially qualified to treat. In what frame of mind, for example, should the Christian read the authors of pagan antiquity? Should he regard paganism and Christianity as irreconcilably opposed—as Swinburne and Shelley regarded them? Or as complementary, as the Renaissance regarded them? Or were the medievals right in thinking that the Christian culture somehow included the classical? Ronald Knox held that there was a measure of truth in each of these attitudes; all three were necessary bookmarkers if the classics were to be read aright. Classical antiquity was sometimes noble with a nobility all its own—the epitaph on the three hundred who died at Thermopylae was a case in point; but it also had its moments of Christian premonition—here Plato's epitaph on Aster seemed to anticipate St. Paul. And, of course, it had its moments of despair. Paganism was "the raw material of our redeemed nature, Christendom in the making." The glory that was Greece and the grandeur that was Rome were not less glorious or less grand if they were seen as Act One in the drama of the Incarnation.

Inevitably the theme of conversion recurs in Ronald Knox's sermons, for here he knew what he was talking about. Conversion was a coming home to a house where everything looked quite different when you got inside. Pressing your nose against the window-pane, you were alarmed by what you saw—or thought you saw—in the lamplit room. The convert was like a prisoner escaped from the wars, bruised and scarred from his difficult trek through the darkness. Knox was appealing for clergymen of the Church of England who had changed their allegiance at much personal cost. "What if *then*, just when a man leans up against a wall to get back his breath, he must be wounded, in that same house, by the viper of poverty and neglect?" Ronald Knox's home-coming had brought its special pain in the knowledge that his father, an Evangelical bishop in the Church of England, would be deeply hurt by his decision. "It was when I was living just across the Severn," he told the congregation assembled for the centenary of the opening of Shrewsbury Cathedral, "that I first conceived those doubts which brought me into the Church. And always, on the further bank of the river, the cathedral of Our Lady Help of Christians stood like an obstinate question-mark. How was I to decide whether it was a beacon-light, or will-o'-the-wisp?" And in another sermon, appropriately named *The Road to Damascus*, he would repeat what he had said in the last sermon he had preached in a Protestant church. His subject was the parting of friends; and, once again, we are reminded of the lonely figure, leaning over the gate at Littlemore.

Divisions, sharper than the sword of earthly jealousies, differences, wider in their estrangment than mere geographical distance, may drift us and them apart; all the comfortable certainties of familiar surroundings we may be called upon to renounce. The past, with its memories, will not be a home to which fancy can return, but a distant harbour at which we have touched, now faded beyond the horizon. To be ready to give up all, houses, and brothers, and sisters, and father, and mother, and lands—that is what it means, to follow Christ.

Ronald Knox was much quicker than Newman to feel at home in his new family; and it is fair to add that the family treated him very much better than they had treated Newman. Whenever one of its more illustrious members died, it was always on the cards that Ronald Knox would be asked to commemorate his passing. And so the panegyrics have a special place in his preaching, for this was a genre in which he particularly excelled. He underlined the point of Chesterton's conversion; that Chesterton "had looked for the thousandth time at the Catholic Faith, and for the first time he saw it." He saw that Belloc was a prophet rather than an apostle, recalling the agitation of Maurice Baring when Chesterton first showed signs of conversion: "Don't tell Hilary," Baring had exclaimed, "he'd ruin everything." Or listen to him on Father Paul Nevill, for more than twenty-five years headmaster of Ampleforth—and Ampleforth was a school to which Ronald Knox was devoted beyond all others, Eton and Shrewsbury excepted.

One of my earliest memories of Ampleforth is standing talking to Father Paul watching a football match; and just in front of us was a small boy who, for no earthly reason, was grinding his heel into the muddy ground and making an ugly brown hole. All that I had ever known of schoolmasters convinced me that it was only a matter of time before a stentorian "Stop doing that, boy!" put an end to the performance. It never came. I realized, with a shock, that the misdemeanour of destroying the grass on the touch-line did not rank high in the new headmaster's scale of priorities.

Not far away, perhaps, on the same football field was the previous headmaster of Ampleforth, now its Abbot—his face, normally drawn and tense, suddenly "lit up with that smile of his that was like a sunny day in winter." Him, too, Ronald Knox would catch with the camera of affectionate insight. But among these panegyrics there is one missing that I should have dearly loved to listen to. Surely no one but Ronald Knox could have done justice to Maurice Baring. Surely no one deserved more richly than Maurice Baring the compliment of a personal tribute—a tribute that the Catholic Church only rarely allows to be paid? A great deal of light is thrown on the character of Ronald Knox when one recalls his casual remark that he was on his way to stay with Maurice Baring, and that he would rather stay with Maurice Baring than with anyone else in the world. For the matter of that, there were not many people he would rather read.

What is it, then, that distinguishes these sermons from others which have held their place in the devotional literature of England? It is, I think, a certain note of familiarity—in the sense that Knox was addressing, and consciously addressing, the members of his own family. He was preaching, if you like, to the converted—even though many of them might need to be converted all over again. (Which of us, indeed, does not?) He presupposed an acquaintance with Catholicism—its doctrines, its idiom, and its history. If the world outside caught the echoes of his voice—as they did, at regular intervals, in *The Sunday Times*—so much the better. But whether he was preaching in Westminster Cathedral or the Brompton Oratory, or in some obscure parish church which had called upon him for a special occasion, he was speaking to his own family—and he did not raise his voice. It was not for him to denounce the sins of society or to engage, militantly, in the controversies of the hour. He would exhort, argue, meditate and persuade; he would not thunder or threaten. But although his sermons were familiar, they were also formal. Not

a comma or a semicolon was out of place. He knew exactly
how much he could fit into the time allotted to him. The
public patience with the pulpit was less than it had been in
Newman's time, much less than it had been in Jeremy Tay-
lor's or Donne's; and so Knox's sermons have neither the
weight, nor the elaboration, of theirs. But what he set out to
do he did to the summit of perfection. For all the scruples of
his style, his aim was not literary but apostolic; he knew how
quickly a facile rhetoric is carried away upon the breeze; and
he was concerned, not that his listeners should be excited but
that they should be saved.

Among the less-known Knoxiana is a fantasy, entitled *The
Rich Young Man*, published by Sheed and Ward in 1928.
This is among the most perfect things he ever did, for the
theme gave equal play to his piety and his imagination. He
conceives a young man inheriting a substantial fortune and
disinclined to share it. One day he comes upon Our Lord
preaching by the lake, asks his casual question, and receives
his disconcerting answer. Time passes; his investments fail; he
takes to fraud, is arrested with a companion in crime, and is
condemned to death. At last the two criminals find themselves
on Calvary with Jesus Christ between them. Then the rich
young man remembers the voice he heard by the lake and
makes the request which is a password to Paradise. The story
is told with an astringent tenderness and a delicate penetration
of human motives. It is prefaced by a characteristic submis-
sion to the judgment of Holy Church in case she should think
his imagination had run away with him!

A comparison between Ronald Knox's sermons and the addresses he gave in retreat shows how exactly he knew how to
measure himself to his audience. The voice is lowered; the
tone is more intimate; the humour peeps out more daringly.

You know that he is sitting in a chair, not standing in a pulpit. Here are a number of people—priests or laymen—gathered together much more deliberately and decisively than people normally gather together for a Sunday Mass or a special ecclesiastical occasion—even when they knew that Ronald Knox was to be the preacher. They were come together, as he put it, to give their souls a spring cleaning, and they will be prepared to work a good deal harder than the ordinary congregation. He, for his part, is there to help them along with a little spiritual technique. And how precise a technique was his! He never, needless to say, talks about himself, never shows himself off; yet there he is, at the end of it all, in the fullness and humility of his priesthood. Not quite as you saw him in the pulpit, or might have listened to him in the confessional, but as if he were talking to you personally, although many others were at your side.

Not many of these addresses were published in his lifetime, for the very practical reason that he was in great demand for Retreats and gave them more than once. In *The Layman and His Conscience* (1961) he covers a remarkably wide range of spirituality, taking his cue from Bartimeus flinging aside his cloak and stumbling forward to meet Our Lord because Our Lord was asking for him. The "grim irony" of Ash Wednesday is vividly brought home:

Just when garden and hedgerow are beginning to put out the first shy promise of green, when the birds are thinking about building their nests, and the mornings grow lighter, and the sun lingers before setting, and there are signs of a fresh vigour in the blood, and we seem to have got rid of the last of our winter colds, and altogether we begin to think things are not so dusty after all, the Church suddenly plucks us by the sleeve and says "Remember, you are dust."

How is the distracted layman to practice the Presence of God? He must proceed gradually, like "an aeroplane taxiing before it can be airborne." How aptly the Crucifix represents the perpetual state of tension between nature and grace! How true that most people don't want to say the Rosary, but to get it said; and how much easier to avoid its monotony if we think of it

as having more or less the shape of a shamrock; with the entrance where the stalk comes, and three circles of rose-bushes in front of us, white ones on the left, for the joyful mysteries, red straight in front of us, for the sorrowful; yellow to the right, for the glorious ones. Each circle has five separate rose-trees in it, and Our Lady's face grows grave or lights up as she shows us one after another, for these are her memories. She will not let us pass through just sniffing the fragrance of them, she will bend down the branches and bring the flowers close to us, so that we can draw a deep breath and drink in the full flavour of the scent.

Now and again, as he draws upon the Gospels, Ronald Knox lets us see the thought behind his own translations. "I beseech you therefore, brethren, by the courtesy of Christ." He confesses his love for the phrase; and only St. Paul would have thought of it. All the translators, except Moffat, had missed it; and Moffat had put "consideration" where he meant "considerateness." It was a quality in which Knox himself was rich, and we are not surprised when he reminds us that

anybody can be kind to children, and get good marks by it, but they can be perfectly happy, really, playing their own games on the floor; it is grandmamma, left in the window-seat with her

knitting and her memories, conscious that people think her rather
a bore, who will be really grateful, even for a word or two.

Knox was perfectly aware of his own gifts, and he admitted to Arnold Lunn that he would rather people disliked
him and admired his translation of the Bible than liked him
and criticized his Bible. So it is interesting to hear him on
humility. Humility didn't require you to revise your opinions,
but it might require you to pocket them. And when you
started a sentence with the words "I do think . . .", it generally meant that you had lost your temper, or were about to
lose it. And so to simplicity—which meant not multiplying
the things you could not do without. St. Benedict Labre had
given up sleeping in the Coliseum, because he was afraid of
becoming too much attached to one particular form of lodg-
ing in the open air, and had taken to other corners of Rome
instead. Ronald Knox did not invite his listeners to sleep out
of doors, but he did invite them, just now and then, to vacate
their favourite armchairs. He would have been the first to
admit that he knew something about attachment to armchairs.
He was not a man for excessive mortification—he once told
me that in Lent he abstained from reading detective stories in
bed—but he lived sparingly for all that. His spiritual muscles
were taut, and how sensitively they vibrated none knew better than those who listened to him in retreat.

His addresses to priests are collected in two volumes: *Retreat for Priests* (1948) and *The Priestly Life* (1958). It is not
for me to discuss the priesthood of Ronald Knox, although
that was the most important thing about him. How deeply he
understood the temptations, the trials, and the opportunities
of his calling these two books eloquently testify. Perhaps the

former is the more interesting. Here he finds an Old Testament text, or prototype, for what he wishes to say. The act of creation leads him on to the grace of ordination; the memory of the Flood to the wise use of creatures—"To the day of his death, Noë never saw a bit of scenery that he liked better than the top of Ararat"; he sees in Joseph the type of Our Lord's Passion, in the crossing of Jordan the passage through death into beatitude, in Saul the reprobated priesthood, and in Moses and Elias on the Mount of Transfiguration "the two great retreatants of the Old Testament." Now and again, though sparingly, metaphor is invoked to illustrate some difficult truth. How to reconcile, for example, Our Lord's acceptance of his Passion with his prayer that the chalice might pass from him?

The storms of emotion which sweep over his passible nature cannot drown the peaceful, resolute accents of his superior will. They beat round the fortress of his being as the waters beat round an immovable rock, and the spray of that impact is the sweat of his agony.

The layman may smile in approbation when he hears his parish priest exhorted to chastise his congregation with whips in the sermon, but not to chastise them with scorpions in the notices. The effect, however, of these addresses, though each carries its reminder of weaknesses to which the clergy may be prone, is not to give any reinforcement to anti-clerical prejudice. They will only heighten the layman's respect for a body of men whom Ronald Knox so humbly, and yet so triumphantly, represented. Knowing their difficulties, he commends them to our charity and our admiration.

10

PROPHECY

IF YOU DO the *Times* crossword every day, it is difficult to remain wholly ignorant of public affairs. You cannot escape the headlines, however eagerly you search for the puzzle which is as important to you as your morning pipe. Now Ronald Knox did the *Times* crossword as regularly as he said the Divine Office, and indeed he claimed to be something of an expert on Printing House Square. He once told me that his researches into who was the most frequent contributor to the correspondence columns left the late Lord Vansittart an easy winner. The stranger might have imagined Ronald Knox as a fugitive scholar, buried in the English countryside; immensely gifted, to be sure, and always to be relied upon to produce the lapidary epigram or the felicitous panegyric; but something of a period piece, wearing, like an old-fashioned Norfolk jacket, the flavour of the lost Balliol generation; something, in fact, of a "Soul."[1] I am not denying that he lent himself, a little, to this caricature. He hated the telephone and detested the metropolis. He did not pretend to be in touch

[1] The name given to a famous coterie of Edwardian intellectuals.

with what he called "the moderns." But, for all that, he was a very exceptional man; and it is the mark of the exceptional man that he does not only what is exceptional in other people, but what is exceptional in himself.

I like to imagine the stacks of a college library fifty or a hundred years hence; perhaps the library of a Catholic college in the United States, because these are the libraries I know best. There, under the appropriate letter, are the works of Ronald Knox—not all of them, but a representative number. The cards inside the cover betray the truth that they are not, nowadays, very much read. The characters and itinerary of *A Spiritual Aeneid* will not say much to a sophomore in Buffalo or Wilkes-Barre in 2020. They do not say much to him today. *Enthusiasm* will have its place in the Seminary, for this is a standard book for specialists. But surely the occasions of the *Occasional Sermons* will seem a little remote in Omaha? And how should the conversations of an Oxford Common Room convey anything whatever to undergraduates who have never set eyes on a don? Nevertheless, there is one book, in this imaginary library of mine, which I fancy will be pretty well thumb-marked, with the salient passages underscored. I have before me, as I write, just such a copy—and it is hard to believe that *God and the Atom* will have lost its relevance fifty years from now, if there is anyone left alive to read it. In a very special sense, it was Ronald Knox's legacy to the world he was so soon to leave.

Like other legacies, it took its beneficiaries by surprise. It was the last book one expected him to have written. It seemed as if the terrible detonation at Hiroshima had, all of a sudden, jolted his psychology into tune with the anxieties of the hour; as if there had opened up before him, now in his later middle age, intellectual possibilities which he had never hitherto envisaged. The Ronald Knox of *God and the Atom* was a new Ronald Knox; his voice had acquired an unfamiliar, a prophetic accent. He had never shown the slightest interest in what is sometimes described as "social Catholicism." He did not share the concern of many English Catholics for the implementation of the Beveridge Report. He had found the regimentations of wartime irksome, even when he admitted them to be necessary. He looked back, not without nostalgia, to the lost liberties of his youth, and he did not anticipate their quick recovery. A naturally law-abiding Englishman, he resented the growing incursions of government, and I doubt if he would have been much consoled by the thought that so many had never had it so good. It would have depended on what you meant by good.

Even where we still hold out against ochlocracy, and enjoy democratic institutions, the shackles of State control tighten round us daily; inspected here, directed there, we find the area of individual choice continually shrinking, our lives increasingly conditioned from above. To discuss the rights and wrongs of all this is no part of my purpose here: all I am concerned to point out is that we are not the *men* we were; in all those daily contacts which make citizens of us, our personalities are being ruthlessly abridged. And where this happens, it is the instinct of a generous nature to build up personality from within, because it has no opportunity to develop outwards.

Many people, even among his closest friends, came to regard Ronald Knox as a man who had given up the world as a bad job; as one whose eyes were fixed on Eternity and who was less and less tempted to fix them elsewhere. He, if anyone

—you felt—was building up his personality from within. So indeed he was; but the personality so built proved to have a quite unexpected power of radiation.

God and the Atom was of course provoked by Hiroshima and it exploded—*via* serialisation in *The Tablet*—with something of the same impact. A bomb had been dropped—and Ronald Knox thought it would have been better if it had not been dropped; or if it had been dropped on a mountain-side instead of on a city. That is as far as he will go in condemnation. He is not a nuclear disarmer. He fully understands the political motives for dropping the bomb—that it would shorten the war and save many Allied lives; but his purpose in discussing the matter is not political at all. Nor, I think, can you say that he is impelled solely by his sense of the supernatural. Equally striking, here, is his sense of history. Something has happened and something has mattered—that is a fair definition of the historic moment. From now on, the world will never be quite the same; a new dimension of danger has been added to our daily lives; undreamt-of possibilities, appalling alternatives, of good and evil have been opened up; God himself, as never before, has been called in question; dazzling progress and utter annihilation starkly confront us—and at the moment when we are within an ace of total victory in a just war, we demonstrate what may well turn out to be the technique of our own destruction. Such were the considerations which prompted Ronald Knox to write his essay. But the interesting and subtle point about the essay is this; that what begins as a rather hesitant complaint about the dropping of the atom bomb ends as a rather eloquent plea for atomic energy. It is worth following the phases of his argument.

It was the scale of Hiroshima which had given the tremendous jolt to our preconceptions. The airman carrying the missile was "the symbol of a catastrophic leap in the history of human achievement." Was not Man, "when he suddenly thus rises above his own level, infringing the prerogative of God himself?" No, that was an illusion, because the inventor was "by definition, only the Hider." Still, might not our ideas about the Hider be considerably changed by the fire we had stolen from him? Might not the shock of a rude discovery set up in the human consciousness a kind of *trauma* which would make belief more difficult than it had been? For the atom bomb had done more than hit Hiroshima. It had hit our sense of cosmic discipline, our complacent optimism, and our trust in the validity of our own moral judgments. The atom, and not only the atom bomb, might well become the totem of twentieth-century atheism. Of what use to plead the argument from design, when design could be so easily upset?

Not for the first time, Ronald Knox found himself longing for a philosopher "with enough courage, enough public standing to undertake the synthesis" between Faith and natural theology and the more frightening aspects of modern knowledge. He did not aspire to such a task himself. "Age has brought me distaste, without bringing me competence, for the arena." But he had returned to the arena, for all that, though with a more limited intention. He set himself to "analyse away the Hiroshima-complex in the minds of well-disposed but muddle-headed people—and perhaps, having analysed, to sublimate it." He was not in the least frightened of the scientists; he only wanted to cure the illusions of their camp-followers. Here, he was helped by his unfailing sense of historical perspective. Lucretius, as he "sounded the Last Post of an unredeemed world in the haunting phrases of his *De*

Rerum Natura," had bridged the centuries and celebrated the Atom "as Pascal, but for the grace of God, might have celebrated it"—though philosophically he had "left it where it was, a lifeless lump of matter, eternally clasping and unclasping its invisible fellows in the toils of a meaningless embrace." And, incidentally, is there any modern poet to whom you could pay the compliment that Ronald Knox paid to Lucretius in saying that he had a "genius for irreligion"? You might say it of Paul Valéry, but of no one else.

It was not a tradition of research but a system of philosophy that the schoolmen had rescued from Greek civilisation, and it was the alchemists—the quasi-magicians—of the late Middle Ages who were really the forerunners of the scientific age. And if you asked what they were working on, Knox replied simply that they were working on the Atom. And so the Grand Canyon of European thought opened up, each generation widening the fissure, with Descartes neglecting "the metaphysical approach because he was lost in contemplating the greatness of the human mind, just as Pascal neglected it because he was lost in contemplating the miseries of the human soul." Had the Atom any but a theoretical importance; and if not, was it worth bothering about? To this question Hiroshima brought the shattering answer. You might almost say that whatever else Hiroshima did, it closed the Grand Canyon. From now on, the scientist and the philosopher were in the same boat—and a boat that was leaking badly. How, for example, would the Thomist proof of ultimate causality stand up to Hiroshima? Ronald Knox seemed to have heard (and no one else would have heard of it) that the foundation of the British railway service was the 10 a.m. train from Kings Cross to York; if that started late, every

other train started late as well. But Hiroshima had opened up
the dreadful possibility of a world in which you could not
believe in Bradshaw. It is not at all difficult, now, to believe in
"a kind of anarchy" at the heart of British Railways; but even
in 1945 the traveller had a few illusions left. When, however,
Knox's hypothetical scientist suggested that there might, after
all, be a kind of anarchy at the heart of nature, he was less
cocksure of the answer than he had been.

If God—even supposing that He exists—is no longer in
control, then you are threatened with a breakdown in the
belief in Divine Providence. Faith having already gone, Hope
will quickly follow. And as for Charity—well, there wasn't a
great deal of Charity in the decision of President Truman. It
wasn't Charity—and speaking as an Englishman, it wasn't
quite cricket either. The unique opportunity had been missed.
A given course of action might have been right, or at least
narrowly justifiable, yet a different course of action might
have been better. "Like David, holding up the piece of cloth
from Saul's garment in the faint light of dawn, we should
have done a better thing by showing the Japanese what we
might have done, and not doing it." And we had released
something more than a single bomb—we had released an impulse of violence and revolt. Thucydides—once again, the
historic past—had noticed how the "long years of the Peloponnesian War had brought with them a deterioration of
public morals; crimes of violence . . . became more frequent
because the conditions of the time had made acts of violence
more familiar." The same thing was happening in post-War
Europe, and Ronald Knox wondered how easy it would be to
imbue the mind of a courageous ex-Commando with the principles of John Stuart Mill. We should be "the slaves of the

Atom, not its masters, if we consent to wear its livery—the livery of explosion and of revolt." What was the use of splitting the Atom—enormous as this triumph might seem—if we ourselves were no more than "fiery particles, bombinating in a world of unrest"?

And so, in the concluding chapters of what is quite a short book, Ronald Knox set about constructing his alternatives to doubt, despair, and decadence. Every generation has its own psychology of belief. For himself, he would probably continue to pray with his eyes shut, looking for God where Kant had told him to look—in the depths of conscience. But might not others look for him, unflinchingly, in the face of his creation? Might not the Atomic Age "re-emphasise the lesson of God's greatness"? Is not this already reflected in a return to the Old Testament on the part of some, in a return to the Early Fathers on the part of others? Let God be terrible, if you will—perhaps we need a reminder of His wrath—let Him be anything but sentimental. The picture of an Omnipotent Creator might not seem so fabulous "to a civilization which holds infinity in the palm of its hand." Natural theology might now come more easily to the modern mind. Moreover, the Christian virtue of hope had "nothing whatever to do with the world's future. As it was preached by the first apostles, it meant nothing more or less than a confidence on the part of the Christian that he or she would attain happiness in a future life. The world about them was perishable, and doomed to perish—in a very short time." This was more readily believed by men in 1945—and in 1960—than by anyone since the time of the Apostles. The Atomic Age and the Apostolic Age have more than a little in common; which accounts, no doubt, within the Church, for a return to the mood of primitive Christianity—or of what primitive Christianity is popularly supposed to have been—and for a certain corresponding distaste for post-Tridentine developments. Ronald Knox does not take one side or the other. He contents himself with suggesting a most valuable analogy between a world almost without hope and a similar condition of near-despair which most of the mystics have known on their way to the Divine Union. The Church had given the verdict to Bossuet in his great quarrel with the Quietists—even in the midst of your despairs, it was your duty to go on hoping. The world of the mid-twentieth century might be storing up for itself such a task of Divine Vengeance as would make the Old Testament look newer than the New. It might be going through a period of purgation which would be the prelude to almost unthinkable achievement and the gradual establishment of Christ's reign on earth. Or it might quite simply be coming to an end. You could bet on one or the other, according as you were optimistically or apocalyptically inclined. But you must not push resignation to the point where hope was extinguished.

This was the answer to despair—the answer of a qualified optimism. But few people had the courage or the lucidity to think through their difficulties to an integral doubt or a total despair. They would prefer to drift in an Atomic cloud of unknowing. They would lack the strength to control the forces they had unleashed, and so the power of their discovery would be dissipated in weakness—or in the violence which is the other face of weakness. This was the temptation of Hiroshima, and it had not been resisted. If it had been resisted, Knox believed that somewhere "a Figure would have bent down from a Cross in salutation." Only religion, he maintained, could make good the Atom's claim to integrate our lives. But "by way of directing man's attention to what religion means and what religion costs" he thought the Allied Powers had "done the next best thing to not dropping a bomb on Hiroshima. They have dropped it." At the time he wrote these words Ronald Knox could not have foreseen the Cheshire Homes; but when he did see them, he may well have slept more easily.

No, he did not regret the splitting of the Atom. Looking back, as he liked to do, to the days when all his world was young, he remembered a school-fellow, Harry Moseley; "unassuming, untidy, inhibited, golden-good, very likeable," whose vague memory still haunted Eton and Trinity. Harry Moseley had been killed at Gallipoli, but not before he had established the relation between the X-ray spectrum and the atomic number. "Would Hiroshima stand, but for him?" You could not set a limit to human discovery, because human discovery was all part of God's revelation of Himself. And so, once again, Ronald Knox asked for the philosopher of his dreams, "one who can thread his way, step by step, through the intricate labyrinth of reasoning into which scientists have been led, eyes riveted to earth, by the desire to improve our human lot, the desire to destroy life, or mere common curiosity; one who can keep his mind, at the same time, open to the metaphysical implications of all he learns, and at last put the whole corpus of our knowledge together in one grand synthesis. He must be able to gaze through the telescope, to peer through the microscope, with a mind unaverted from that great Source of all being who is our Beginning and our last End." At the same time, we needed "an acceleration in the tempo of our spiritual reactions, to meet and match what must

surely be an acceleration of tempo in the material developments of history." And so he hoped for the Saint.

Was he asking for the moon? He himself would forbid us
to assume so. Not long after he committed that plea to paper,
I had the privilege of meeting Pierre Teilhard de Chardin in
the Maison des Etudes in Paris. He had just returned from
China to a France reeling under the shock of Hiroshima, to
which incidentally he had been closer than we were. We
talked through a long summer afternoon. He did not speak in
a terminology of which I should have understood nothing,
and his mere presence—at once patrician and apostolic—his
infectious courage, his radiant intelligence were, for all of us
gathered there in the little garden of the Rue Monsieur,
antidotes to despair. Technically, I suppose, Teilhard was
neither a philosopher nor a theologian, but he was a poet and
a priest, a scientist and a seer. Ronald Knox was severe on
premature attributions of sanctity; but you could no more
question the spirituality of Teilhard de Chardin than you
could question the spirituality of Ronald Knox. In these matters sinners have always had a vote. And if you read *The
Phenomenon of Man* and *The Divine Milieu* alongside of
God and the Atom, you will surely find in Teilhard de
Chardin something of the synthesis, and much of the spirituality, that Ronald Knox was so prophetically seeking. Here,
at least, was a voice to which the atomic century is prepared
to listen. How far the caution of the one would have accom-
panied the intrepidity of the other is a guess that I am not
competent to hazard. But I shall always remember the light in
Teilhard's face and the undaunted emphasis in his voice as he
answered our doubts—"il faut *croire*." And for Ronald Knox
that was always the heart of the matter.